SABRINA

SABRINA

The Autobiography of a Cat

As dictated to

Michelle Russell

Catsong Publishing
Grand Rapids, Minnesota

Visit: http://www.catsongpublishing.com

Second Printing 2014; First Printing 2008

Published by
Catsong Publishing
33034 Crystal Springs Road
Grand Rapids, MN 55744
Catsong2@netzero.net

Russell, Michelle
    Sabrina, The Autobiography of a Cat
    Includes bibliographical references, appendix and index
    ISBN: 978-09800642-7-8
    Library of Congress Control Number: 2014919350

2014 edit: Michelle Russell
2014 interior: Marny K. Parkin
Original edit: H. Michele Thomas, Esq., M.A., and Christine Russell
Cover design: Nanette Villaneuva
Original interior Design: Kyle Laule

All photos excepting below copyright © Michelle Russell
Back cover photo copyright © 1996 Tom & Marie Hegeman
Nancy LaMott photo courtesy of Stephen Mosher © 1990

Printed in the United States of America

To All Pet Lovers

Contents

A Note and Special Thanks

Over the last six years, Sabrina's book has been well-loved by all who read it. During this same time, there have been numerous changes in publishing, so it seems only right that this year a new edition be released. It is my hope that many new readers will have the chance to know Sabrina's story.

Although, *Sabrina* is essentially the same book it was in 2008, I have taken the liberty of sprucing it up a bit without my dear Sabrina's presence. In addition, some new dietary notes have been made. I don't think Sabrina will mind. For those purchasing an e-book, we have found it necessary to cut back on the number of photos. Copies of the original book are still available, along with the new edition.

As noted in the original release, Sabrina wanted to express her deepest thanks to Doris Day and the *Doris Day Animal League* for their tireless efforts on behalf of the animals. Sabrina and I are both grateful for DDAL's sympathy and desire to help in the days following Elizabeth's abduction. The efforts to prevent animal cruelty in our world are of great importance.

My personal thanks to those who supported this work in its early days: C.B. Arnette, Christine Russell, Michele Thomas and Kyle Laule, who created the original interior design. Additional thanks goes to Stephen Mosher for the use of his Nancy LaMott photograph, the Professional Photography Studio of Wilkes Barre, Pennsylvania, and Nannette Villaneuva for her superb cover. Many thanks to Marny Parkin for her work on the photographs and design in this new edition.

November 2006
White Haven,
Pennsylvania

Dear Reader:

Here I sit, curled up in my favorite, red leather-backed chair, ready to dictate the story of my life. I know some of you won't believe a cat could write a book, but I assure you the words and opinions here are entirely mine.

I also must tell you it was not my idea to write this book. Cats do not think of writing books. No, it was my human mother who convinced me to tell my story—for I have lived a long and interesting life.

Once I was young and beautiful. I lived in Washington, D.C. Now, I am old and tired. Sometimes, I even have trouble walking across the room.

So let me begin my tale. I hope you enjoy it. In the end, you know, it really is a story of love.

Sincerely,
Sabrina

My First Picture

Chapter 1
My Beginnings

I was born in Washington, D.C. in May of 1987. Of course, I don't remember that, nor do I remember my cat mother or my brothers and sisters. They are only shadowy dreams to me.

My first memory is of being alone in a garden. There was a jungle of grass and plants towering over me. And I was so tiny, all I could do was cry in my loudest voice, "Meooow! Help! Mother, where are you?"

A very nice lady came along and I heard her say, "Oh, my! Look at this tiny little kitten! Where is her mother?" At the time, I really didn't know what she was saying, but I was glad to be found.

The lady picked me up and took me to her home, where she fed me warm milk. Then she made me a bed in a little box with towels. It was there I slept, warm and secure, for what seemed many days.

It would be difficult to say how long I stayed in this home, but somehow I knew this woman was not going to be my permanent mother. Still, she took very good care of me and gave me a lot of love. Before long, I had grown to nearly twice the size I was when the lady found me.

One day, a young man with curly red hair and a happy laugh came to the lady's home. It was clear he was quite pleased with me. He packed me in a box and took me off to a new home.

When I emerged from the box, I was in a sunny yellow room with soft brown carpet and large pieces of gray furniture. This bright room led to a smaller room where there were tall, orange platforms that seemed to go up in the air. Yes, people call them "stairs." These stairs were far too big for me to climb, and I felt a bit lost.

"Here, kitty, kitty," said the man with the red hair. I followed him through a rather dark area, into a yellow room with bumpy yellow flooring. At the end of that room there was a big space in the wall where the outside light came through.

The man laid a piece of paper in the center of the floor. On this paper he put a bowl of clear substance called "water" and another bowl with big, hard things that smelled good. Then the man with the red hair, having shown me my food and a box for my toilet use, left the room and disappeared.

After the man left, I sniffed the plate. I had never seen anything like the big, solid brown things. Because of their appetizing odor, I tried to lick and even tried to chew them, but I soon gave up.

Suddenly, I felt quite scared, so I ran as fast as I could into the sunny front room and hid under the largest piece of furniture I could find. Soon, I was fast asleep.

The next thing I remember was a noise at the door. There was a jangle of keys and the sound of human footsteps. In my young years, I was fearless, so boldly I crawled out from under the furniture and walked toward the giant lady who had entered the house. Looking up at her, I cried out, "Mew! Mew!"

"Oh, baby," she said, picking me up in a gentle way that told me she knew about kittens. "You are too small to be away from your mommy!"

Later, I would hear her tell Lindsay (for that was the name of the nice young man with the curly red hair) that I was too young and should go back to my mother. To this, Lindsay replied, "She doesn't have a mother. She's been without a mother for a long time."

Yes, it was sad but true. I had been thrust out into the world too early, but somehow, I had survived. As a tiny baby, I learned how to fend for myself, or at least make others listen to me.

The nice young lady took me into the kitchen and started to prepare a meal for me. I guess she knew from the way I was crying that I was very hungry. Lindsey meant well, but the food he laid out for me was bigger than my mouth.

"Oh, baby," the lady said when she saw the food, "You can't eat that! You don't have any teeth to chew it!" Later, she scolded Lindsay about my food, but of course, he didn't know any better.

Michelle (which, as I soon learned, was the lady's name) warmed some milk for me. Then, while I was busy lapping it up, she began cooking chicken in a pot with carrots and other things. For the next several weeks, chicken broth would be my only food, and I lapped it up happily, purring all the while, until my little tummy was full and fat.

At night, my new mommy, Michelle, carried me up the stairs and down a long hallway to her small bedroom at the back of the house. There, she put me on the foot of her bed, but as soon as she lay down, I ran mewing to the top of the bed to be near her. No matter how many times she sent me to the foot of the bed, I would run back up to her pillow, crying "Mew! Mew!" Finally, she let me curl up beside her, but I was sneaky. As soon as Michelle was asleep, I found a way to crawl under the covers. Once I was there, I rolled myself into a tiny ball, where I lay all night, nice and warm, next to my new mommy. And so it was every night.

My new human mother seemed to know how a cat mother makes her kittens grow healthy and strong. She would stroke my head, my ears, my back, my tummy and all my little feet while I rolled 'round and 'round, enjoying the entire experience. This was love, and aside from food, love is really what makes all babies grow.

So, the days in my new home on Capitol Hill went from spring to steamy summer and, then, to golden fall. And as the months passed, I grew in happiness and size from a tiny kitten to a medium-sized kitten. In fact, for the first year of my life, my name was "Kitten"!

At the front door of our home on "G" Street

Chapter 2
Life on "G" Street

For the first eight years of my life, I lived in Washington, D.C. in an old two-story brick townhouse on Capitol Hill. I know the house was old because sometimes a lady leading a group of tourists with an umbrella would stand outside and talk about Abraham Lincoln and such. I didn't know who that was, but my mother says it meant our house was very old (probably built before the Civil War, around 1860).

Our house was a happy home, and it seemed as if it had always been happy, for there were no dark shadows or spirits lurking there, only sunny ones.

The house was long from front to back and, although I was not allowed to go outside by myself, there was plenty to do inside. In the mornings, I would sleep upstairs in Michelle's bed. Then in the afternoon, I would head down-stairs to play with my ball, and look out the windows at the neighborhood birds and squirrels going about their daily routines. After that, it was time for a catnap on the large, gray chair, which sat just below the big window in the front parlor. In the afternoon, the sun came through this window, making it the perfect spot for sunbathing.

Our house sat on a little hill above the sidewalk. Just inside the gate separating the yard from the sidewalk were four iron steps built into the earth. These steps went up to a landing and a small garden in which I liked to play. There was a tree with a climbing rose vine growing over it. Once a year, this vine bloomed in a waterfall of red roses. Later, my mother would plant bluebells, tulips and yellow buttercups in this garden.

Sabrina in her window

From the garden, another set of iron steps led up to the front door. We could always tell when someone was approaching the door by the sound of their footsteps on these stairs. The house was built quite a ways above the street. Consequently, from my spot on the gray chair in the front window, I had a perfect view of "G" Street and all its "comings and goings."

Each day, I would sit in the window, watching people walk by as I awaited Michelle's return from work. From my perch, I was able to see her coming down the block and, after a while, I knew exactly what time she would appear. As she opened the front gate, she would always look up at the window and laugh to see me sitting there. Our eyes would meet and I would arch my back and meow.

When Michelle came through the door, I was always there to greet her. She would pick me up and kiss me. Then, I would run to the kitchen, where she gave me my dinner. Whether she arrived home on time or late, we always had the same routine.

After dinner, it was time to play. I would run from room to room, and, when my legs got longer, up and down the stairs like a maniac. My favorite game was trying to chew the cord on the bamboo window shade, but Mom took the cord away from me, saying she was afraid I would hang myself. On other occasions, with nothing better to do, I would walk up my mother's left arm, across her back and down the right arm. Riding on her shoulder was another great trick, but of course, only when I was small. Despite my momentary lapses into crazy kittenhood, I was, for the most part, a lady.

At this point in my story, it seems a good time to describe my appearance. I suppose some might call me a tabby. However, to my mother's pride and my own, I was not an ordinary striped tabby. I was completely black on top and on my sides, instead of stripes, I had swirls of flecked gray and black. My legs were gray with thick black lines of varying shape and size. My underside was flecked gray. I had no white. My eyes were green, rimmed in black with lighter fur around them. My nose, which was orange, was also outlined in black. As I grew older, the light shading of my face and body grew darker. In the sun, however, my fur appeared almost chocolate colored. I knew I was an exotic cat because everyone who saw me remarked upon my deep, dark, rich coat and my green eyes.

I was considered a small cat. Once I was grown, my weight remained typically between seven and eight pounds. As for my shape, I was long and thin, and I am proud to say I have kept a good figure throughout my life. Yes, I have always been considered quite a beauty.

My mother liked to have me around when she was doing various things, whether it was cleaning, gardening or taking a bath. By the time I was half-grown, she noticed something unusual about me. Unlike most cats, I wasn't afraid of water. If it were raining outside (and rain in Washington, D.C. can be quite intense), I would not even hesitate about going out. And if I was already outside when it began to rain, I seldom thought about coming back in.

Sometimes in the evening, when Michelle was running her bath, I would stand on my hind legs and watch the water going into the tub. She liked to put bubble bath in the water, and this fascinated me. I would sit on the edge of the tub and try to bat the bubbles to see if I could catch them.

One night, Michelle took me in to the bathroom with her, and since it was not unusual for me to sit on the edge of the tub, she didn't think much about my sitting there while she bathed. On this particular night, she was sitting toward the front of the tub, leaving a lot of space with bubbles behind her. Since it looked fun, I decided to join her. I took flying leap.

Splash! I was in the tub, swimming in all those bubbles. I was quite shocked. It was not at all what I had expected. Before I knew what had happened, Michelle reached around, grabbed me and pulled me out. For the first time in my life, I was sopping wet.

"Oh, Kitten!" my mother said. "Now look what you've done!"

I guess I looked like a drowned mouse. My mom had to wash all the bubble bath off me and then wrap me in a towel so, as she put it, I "would not catch my death of cold." Since it was night and there was no sunshine to help dry my fur, Mom proceeded to give me a rubdown. I was not pleased about that and decided I would not go for a bathtub swim again. Well, it was fun for a moment.

Another day, I was taking my usual walk from the living room into the hall when suddenly, out of the corner of my eye, I saw something unusual. In fact, it was so strange looking, I actually shot up in the air about two feet. After I realized the object wasn't moving, I crept over to it slowly and carefully to check it out.

It was an odd looking thing with a flat bottom covered in carpet, and a long, round trunk rising up from the ground like a tree, also covered in carpet. I thought. "What is this?" My mother explained, and I soon caught on. This strange object was for scratching and exercising my toes. I was to use this instead of using the carpet, the stairs or the furniture. A scratching post of my very own? I liked that! Still, with my cat's nature, I knew if I ever wanted to get a rise out of my mom, all I had to do was give a little scratch or two to the stairs. Then, I better run as fast as I could! I'll have you know, though, that I have always been a lady, even in my young years, and this behavior almost never happened.

In addition to my mother's love for me, I knew that Lindsay was also quite fond of me. I used to love it when he held me mid-air with one hand under my front legs, while he stroked me from head to tail in one long sweep with the other hand. He would laugh, and I would smile. I know he thought I was a beauty and was very proud of me. I was pretty proud of myself. Often in the evenings, when Lindsay was watching television, we would spend time together.

Lindsay and our other roommate, Dan, seemed to enjoy my company, though I must say, sometimes they seemed to be mostly interested in ruffling me up. They liked to drink beer and put the beer can tabs on my tail.

"Don't you dare put those tabs on that cat's tail," Michelle would tell them.

"She likes it!" they would laugh.

"She does not! Don't do it again!"

In those days, I was so young and innocent, I went along with the game. I was glad to have a home and someone to play with. My mother, however, seemed insistent that I receive only the best treatment.

Life continued on "G" Street. I had my first visit to Jane's Veterinary, got my shots and proved to be growing into a healthy, happy cat. The only remaining problem, though I didn't see it as a problem, was my name. I was still just "Kitten."

Chapter 3
I Become a Mother

Time passed quickly, and soon, I became an adult. In cat years, we are considered an adult by nine months or one year. By the time I reached this age, the young tomcats of the neighborhood began to hang around and court me.

Behind our house was a brick courtyard, which we shared with the house attached to ours. The ground of this courtyard was covered almost entirely in brick, with two exceptions. The first was a small patch of land to the back on one side of the yard. The second was a small circle of earth in the center of the yard, where a huge, old pear tree stood. The courtyard was surrounded by brick and wood fencing in the back and a combination of block and wood fencing on the sides.

Generally, I was allowed to play in the courtyard by myself on Saturday and Sunday afternoons. I liked to scratch my claws on the wooden fence and then settle down on the brick wall to enjoy the smell of the leaves and, on occasion, the smell of our neighbors' dinners. From the wall, I was also able to observe the small gardens of the neighborhood and watch their goings on.

Beyond the gardens was an alley shared by the entire block. It was there that many cats roamed and met one another. In those days, my Mom was very busy and had no idea where or how I spent my time outdoors.

Less than a year after I came to live on "G" Street, my belly began to grow fat. At first I had only little bumps on my sides, but then those bumps began to swell. One day, my mom looked at me and said, "Oh Kitten! Are you going to have babies?" Lindsay, who was sitting near by came over to look at me and said, "Yes, she is."

I felt quite proud of myself, but I really didn't know all that was involved in motherhood. Day by day and week by week, my stomach grew until it became uncomfortable for me to lie down. Before long, as I lay sunning myself in the front parlor, I could feel the babies moving about inside. The only question now was—when would I give birth?

Each night, I made my way up the stairs, down the long hallway, to the back bedroom and onto my mother's soft, comfortable bed. Each morning, as my mother got ready for work, I made my way down the hall and, with my big stomach swinging from side to side, down the stairs, through the dining room, into the kitchen for breakfast.

There was one morning, however, when I simply didn't feel like getting out of bed. My mother noticed this and, on the way out the door to her job on Capitol Hill, she said, "Kitten, are you all right?"

I purred, putting my head back down on the pale turquoise comforter with the pink rosebuds and closed my eyes. It was peaceful in that back room. The only sounds I heard were those of the birds singing in the pear tree outside.

Then suddenly, I felt quite ill. It seemed the whole world was erupting in my tummy. I found my way under the comforter and waited. I remember the house was so quiet that day; there was no one to hear my cries as the babies pushed their way out.

Around noon, my mother made an unexpected return. She was worried because I had not come down to breakfast that morning. When she returned home, I was not in my usual place downstairs, nor was I on the bed upstairs. Only the cries of my new babies gave away our hiding place.

As my mother turned back the quilt and saw us lying there, I was truly afraid of what she thought. We had made a terrible mess on top of her flannel nightgown. In addition, instead of just me, there were now five kittens! But immediately, she seemed pleased.

"Oh Kitten!" she said, "You had your babies!" Gently, she ran her fingers over the tiny babies nursing at my breasts.

"They are beautiful!" she told me, and I purred.

After a moment, Michelle gasped. I knew the reason. Looking at the babies, she realized who the father was, and it wasn't the cat she had expected!

For the last month, there had been a big question about who the babies' father was. There was a very handsome, orange cat that came to court me. He would sit outside, calling to me, smiling and rubbing his head on the cement. He looked very much the part of "Romeo," while I, sitting in my balcony—the open window above him—looked very much the part of "Juliet." My orange "Romeo" smiled at me, as I rubbed my head against the window frame. I was quite taken with him. He was charming, and I enjoyed his company. For a while, he came to see me almost every day. Because of this, naturally, everyone thought he was the father of my children.

Meanwhile, Lindsay and Michelle had been busy rehearsing for a play. The rehearsals were taking place in the producer's home, which was "kitty-corner" from us. This home on Sixth and "G" Street Southeast was a grand brick house, originally built in the 1800s as a residence for the Mayor of Washington, D.C. It never did become the Mayor's residence, but it was certainly the biggest house in the neighborhood.

The owner of this home, Mrs. "M" had a very big white cat named Jupiter. In fact, as my mother later learned, just three weeks prior to the birth of my kittens, Mrs. "M" had taken poor Jupiter to the vet to be "fixed" with the hope that it would stop his tom-catting ways.

Imagine my mother's surprise then when she turned back the covers and discovered amongst my five kittens, three white ones looking exactly like Jupiter! Yes, I had mated with the richest cat in the neighborhood.

The birth announcement of Jupiter's and my children was made that day, both at Mom's job, a Congressional Office on Capitol Hill, and at the rehearsal of the play. On both occasions, I understand, the news was received with applause. Of course, everything I did was top!

I was quite happy being a mother.

I was quite happy as a mother. Caring for my five kittens was one of the most satisfying and tranquil periods of my life. Because I was such an exotic cat, some may not have pictured me in such a domestic role, but I actually enjoyed it. However, I do have to say, it was quite a big job to ensure that these five kittens were raised properly.

Kittens grow up very quickly, and by the time my babies were seven or eight weeks old, my mother explained that she could not keep all my children. She assured me, however, that all of them would go to very good homes.

As much as I loved my babies, by this time they had become something of a burden. I remember how tired I was trying to feed them all. So, one by one, they each went to new homes. It was an adjustment for me. After each one left, I cried and went around the house searching for my baby until I realized they were truly gone. One of the white girls went to live with her father, and the two who looked like me got homes very quickly.

Then, I had only two kittens left—a boy and a girl. The little white boy was ten weeks old when he finally got a home. The little girl was my favorite, and my mother decided to keep her. Now, I would have a companion and not be alone so much of the time. My mother named my little girl Elizabeth.

Elizabeth was a beautiful and loving girl, all white, except for a black swirl on the top of her head. Her father had a similar swirl, but his was orange.

Elizabeth and I got on very well. I would clean her face, and she would clean mine. There was not a mean bone in her body. She was as friendly to people as she was to other animals. She greeted visitors to our home far better than I did. I liked people, but I was not overly friendly.

Elizabeth did have one very odd habit. She loved socks. Sometimes, the men of our house left their dirty socks, or even their newly laundered ones, in a pile on the floor. Later, when no one was around, Elizabeth went around collecting socks. She'd take them and put them in a pile somewhere in the house. I remember Dan coming out of his room one day and saying, "Where are my socks?" Well, Elizabeth had them.

My daughter Elizabeth was very smart too. It was dark one day when my mother came home. As she came in the door, she pushed the light switch up to turn the living room lights on. I had been sleeping on the couch, and Elizabeth was sound asleep on the chair by the door. After my mom turned the lights on, Elizabeth got up and pulled the light switch down, turning the lights off. Then, she lay down and went back to sleep. My mother was quite astounded at this.

With my daughter as my companion, the days at home were much less lonely. Elizabeth and I passed our time together happily—perfect companions.

Lindsay and Me

Chapter 4
I Receive My Name

Now that I was fully-grown and a mother, the question of my name came up once again. I remember Lindsay and Dan watching television one night, and Lindsay saying, "Kitten really must have a name! "Kitten" is not a name."

"I agree," said my mother, "She has outgrown her name."

The guys came up with a variety of names that are usually given to animals, names like: Fluffy, Fido, Furball, and the like. My mother made it quite clear that I needed a nice "people" name.

Then, one day a short time later, Lindsay and Dan were watching a television game show, and I was sitting on the floor with them.

"Alright," said Lindsay. "Let's make a deal. The next name we hear on the show will be Kitten's new name."

My mother was working in the kitchen, not paying much attention to what the guys were saying.

"Alright," she said and then walked out of the room and up the stairs. On her return, I heard Lindsay say, "Okay! We have a name! Are you ready?" Then, laughing in his usual way, he said, "It's Murdes! Kitten's new name is going to be Murdes!"

My mother was indignant!

"You are not going to call that beautiful cat Murdes," she declared.

Over the next day or two, Lindsay tried to call me Murdes, but I ignored him. I knew my name as "Kitten," and was satisfied with that. Besides,

I didn't like the sound of "Murdes." Lindsay then tried other names on my mother, but to each one she said, "No! No!"

Finally, several weeks later, Lindsay was again watching television in the dining room with me sitting by his side. Suddenly, he called out, "I've got it! I've got Kitten's new name!"

My mother came into the room and said, "What?"

"Sabrina!"

Lindsay was watching the movie *Sabrina* with Audrey Hepburn. Of course, Sabrina is a beautiful name, and Audrey Hepburn was a person similar to the kind of cat I am. My mother was pleased with my new name, and I was as well. It stuck. I started answering to "Sabrina" right away. That was me!

So, that is how, after I was already a year old, I received the name I have carried for nearly nineteen years.

Chapter 5
Elizabeth & the Men Who Steal Pets

In July of 1988, shortly after I received my new name, I went to the doctor and had an operation. Although I didn't quite understand what had happened to me at the time, I felt that something had changed and I wasn't sure I was very happy about it. In the long run, this operation meant that I would not have any more kittens. Perhaps this was part of my personality change toward other cats in the future, for my personality did change, and not for the better. But I am getting ahead of myself.

Now, as I've said before, life at 516 "G" Street, SE in Washington, D.C. was quite happy. I was living with Elizabeth, Michelle, Lindsay, and Dan. Then, Dan moved back to California and another roommate, Rodney, moved in.

With three people in the house, there was always someone there to feed us and see how we were. Sometimes, Michelle would go away for a night or even several weeks. During these times, Lindsay took care of us. Sometimes, he even had us in his room. But besides the need for someone to feed us and occasional companionship, we cats pretty much lived our own lives.

At night, Elizabeth and I usually stayed with Michelle, sleeping on her single bed in the small room at the end of the hall. We were very attached to her. When she had surgery and had to stay in bed for several days, we kept watch over her like two nurses. I stayed with her while Elizabeth took a break, and then Elizabeth stayed while I took a break. We knew things were not quite right, and of course, we would never leave her alone under those circumstances.

By the spring of 1989, Elizabeth was a grown-up cat. On one of her out-ings, the "call of the wild" came over her. That day, when she came home, she walked up to me in her usual way to give me a kiss. As soon as I took one sniff of her face, I knew exactly what she had been up to. I drew back my paw and slapped my beautiful daughter across her face. She was very surprised, but I could not accept the fact that she had been with a tomcat.

I had expected her to be faithful to me. I suppose it couldn't be helped. She was bound to find a mate, but I didn't like it. This event signaled the end of our mother-daughter relationship. After this, I found I did not want her near me. We went on living together, but things were never quite the same.

A few weeks after this event, we celebrated the first anniversary of Eliza-beth's birth (March 13, 1988). Michelle decided to have a party for Elizabeth and invited her friend from work, Sue, who brought her cat, Sarina, to join us. With a strange cat in the house, Elizabeth and I bonded together once more, sitting on the big, black cabinet by the kitchen window. We remained in that spot for most of the evening. Elizabeth received a cake with one candle, and Mom took pictures of us. It was a nice party.

Since Elizabeth was now fooling around with tomcats, it was not too long before there was a box of mewing kittens in my mother's room.

Hoping, no doubt, that my heart would soften and my mothering instinct return at the sight of my grand-kittens, Mom showed me the little, furry balls. I had been such a happy mother she could not imagine me being anything but pleased. Yet the sight of those kittens made me furious. I did not want them anywhere in the house and certainly not anywhere near me. As far as I was concerned, we were being invaded by cats, and I didn't like it! I had been happy with things just as they were.

Elizabeth, to her credit, was a very loving mother. As a daughter, she never held any grudges toward me. She was always open to resuming our relationship, and there were a few moments when I softened enough to sit with her, or at least allow her peaceful presence near me.

I know my mother looked on me with horror. But what most people don't understand is cats' ways are not the same as people's ways. Once those cute little, white and black babies began running about playing, I was filled with even greater rage! If one of them came my way, "Pow!" I would smack it, just as I would any other cat.

There was a day when I actually hit one of those little kittens, knocking it down. It had run up to me, and I didn't want it near me. I can still remember the line of innocent little faces looking at me with awe and fright as my mother grabbed me angrily and forced me to face them. But even my mother's anger would not change my feelings or soften my attitude. I hated those little, running things with a passion.

During that time, I think my mother considered me a hateful cat. She wondered what had happened to the sweet girl I had been—the cat she loved so much. She may even have considered sending me away. We loved one another, but it was a very difficult time. I hissed at Elizabeth; I hissed at the kittens; I even hissed at Michelle. Finally, my solution was to avoid the whole group by spending most of my time upstairs in the bedroom.

Eventually, the kittens grew and found other homes—all except one. In the end, my mother did for Elizabeth what she had done for me—she let Elizabeth keep one of her children, the last one; a little girl kitten. Of course, this made Elizabeth happy, for as I have said, she was a very loving cat and did not like being alone.

Elizabeth & her kittens

The kitten who stayed was a shy, white girl with two dark curls in the center of her forehead. My mother thought she was delicate and sweet like the Japanese cherry blossoms that bloom in Washington, D.C. each spring. So, she named her Blossom.

Blossom was very much a scaredy-cat, and as she grew up this trait grew worse. She was afraid of people and would cry if someone approached her. The only way she let my mother pet her was if she herself had gone to my mother first. On her own terms, Blossom was very affectionate.

As much as she was afraid of people, Blossom loved other cats and approached them easily. She often tried to approach me, but in time, she realized that we would never be close. All the same, she was loving and good-natured. I truly never saw her respond in anger to any one.

Blossom adored her mother, Elizabeth, and the two spent all their time together. Meanwhile, I went on with my solitary life. My motto was: "I like people, but I don't like cats." In fact, odd as it may seem, I actually preferred small dogs to cats! If I met a little dog, I sniffed noses with it. I never hissed or attacked a dog. If a dog started barking at me, I just sat and stared at him.

Blossom

For some time after Blossom joined our family, the house remained peaceful. While I was not interested in having a relationship with my daughter or granddaughter, I loved meeting Lindsay and Rodney's friends whenever they came to visit. After greeting their guests, I would sit on the back of the couch and watch the goings on. During this time, Michelle and Lindsay had a big party, but unfortunately, I was not invited. They felt it would be safer if I were locked away.

In the autumn of 1989, my mother went to Paris for ten days. When she returned, Elizabeth was pregnant again. Mom said she had not intended for this to happen, but there it was. This time, Elizabeth had five long-haired kittens—three white, one orange, and one tabby. My mother thought maybe Elizabeth had mated with a Persian cat, though we didn't know of any Persian cats in the neighborhood.

By the time these kittens arrived, Rodney had moved out, and we had moved into the middle bedroom, which was almost twice the size of our former room. Living in this room, there was a lot more space for all of us.

I was now resigned to accept the fact that once again there were kittens in the house, and my mother was resigned to the fact that I was not going to like them. In the evenings, I sat peacefully on one corner of the bed, while Elizabeth took care of her kittens on another part of the bed.

Blossom seemed quite pleased with her mother's new babies and acted as nursemaid to them. She liked to clean them and take care of them as if they were her own. It was a great help to Elizabeth because she didn't have to worry so much about where the kittens were or if they were in trouble. It was also good because during this time, Elizabeth became ill.

At the time, the kittens were about three or four weeks old and still dependent on their mother for feeding. Elizabeth, who had always suffered from a delicate stomach, suddenly became ill and was unable to keep any food down. She was giving her all to feed these very chubby kittens, but without food, she weakened quickly. After a day or so, she became terribly thin and weak. Michelle took her to Jane's Veterinary Hospital, and the vet said Elizabeth needed to stay in the hospital for at least two days in order to regain her strength and get her stomach working properly.

When Michelle came home without Elizabeth, we were all rather worried. How were these kittens going to get along without their mother? Somehow, Michelle figured out how to feed them, and Blossom did the rest, cleaning them and taking care of them during the night. The next evening, Elizabeth returned home well-rested and picked up where she left off. She was now able to continue mothering her babies without destroying her health.

After a few more weeks, the kittens had grown enough to go on to new homes. Because it was autumn, all of them got good homes quickly, with the exception of a little, white kitten with an orange spot on her head. This little girl was promised to Michelle's mother in California. She had to wait to go to her new home until Michelle traveled there for Christmas. Meanwhile, Blossom and Elizabeth were glad to have this little girl at home with

Polly and her sister

them. This kitten really looked like a Persian cat. Imagine—all three of my descendents in the house were white!

Once the kitten got to California, Michelle's mother, Marian, named her "Polly" for politics since she was a Washington, D.C. cat. Eventually, Polly became the wife of the Prefontaine cat, Henry, and they lived happily together for many years. But more about Polly later.

Once Baby Polly was gone, Elizabeth continued to be happy because she had Blossom. A short time after Polly left, my mother took Elizabeth to the vet and had her fixed so there would be no more kittens. She also took Blossom. "Too many cats need homes," she said. "We don't need more babies."

During all these years, my Mom continued to cook for us on a fairly regular basis. She would make a big pot of Jewish Chicken Soup, which I loved. She always said it was one thing that kept me healthy. Then, once in a while, she would try something else out on us.

I remember one time she made me a plate of something. It looked like chicken, but it wasn't. Elizabeth was eating it, but I just couldn't; so I walked out of the kitchen, through the dining room and into the hall leading upstairs. Mom followed me. She was unhappy with the fact that I hadn't eaten.

"Sabrina," she said, "It's turkey. It's just like chicken!"

I gave her a look to kill, shook my head, stuck out my tongue and ran full-speed up the stairs. "Turkey like chicken? The heck it is!"

❧

Now and then on weekends and late afternoons, when it was warm, we were allowed to go out. However, we were always expected to come home at night and stay indoors when everyone was at work.

As I said before, our neighborhood on Capitol Hill was very old. Most of the houses had been there at least a hundred years. They were built in various styles and stood close to one another, with small gardens in front and small fenced yards in the back. Behind the backyards were paved alleys, where some residents parked their cars.

Once outdoors, I would sharpen my claws on the wooden fence and then climb onto the brick wall. I stayed up there for hours; walking along the wall and sitting in different locations. Sometimes, I'd sneak down into the yards on the other side, but I soon learned this was not so wise because there might be a dog in one of those yards, or even a cat that wanted to fight. Sitting on the brick wall or the roof of the small garage behind us, was one of my favorite things to do. From there, I was able to survey the entire neighborhood and enjoy the outdoors without being disturbed.

In the spring, our lovely old pear tree was full of white blossoms. In summer, it was thick with leaves that shaded our yard. In the fall, the tree was filled with a hundred ripe pears, which the squirrels loved to eat. I was fascinated by these squirrels, and my mother, noticing this, often had to remind me: "Sabrina, stay away from the squirrels! You'll get fleas!" I guess she said that because the squirrels were always scratching themselves.

Together, Elizabeth and I had many pleasurable hours outdoors. Our outings were especially good on summer evenings when we could escape the heat of the house. If you can imagine being in a pot of steaming chicken soup, then you will know just how hot and steamy D.C. could be. At night, it was no cooler. If anything, it was worse. The old bricks of our house seemed to absorb the heat of the day, turning our home into a brick oven.

It was just such a day in June of 1990; a day I will never forget. It was the most terrible day of my life. The day started as a beautiful, but very hot day. When evening arrived, our mother let us out to sit in the brick courtyard under the old pear tree, and cool off. We had all been sitting around the back door, enjoying the cool air—Elizabeth, Blossom and I. Mom brought us in for a while, but because of the terrible heat indoors, she let us go out once more. Blossom stayed close to the door, but Elizabeth and I wandered off to the back of the yard and out to the alley.

Elizabeth always did like to wander. She was so friendly to people that she would often sit on the brick wall in the front of the house and greet the neighbors as they walked by. She even allowed total strangers to pet her. Alas, this was to be her downfall.

I was there, and I saw what happened. They waited in the back of the alley—those men who steal animals and do terrible things to them. They put a wire noose around your neck and slip you away so quickly as you choke and squirm, that you cannot cry or get loose.

Just as it happened, my mother called us. Terrified, I ran with all my might into the house. Maybe, they wanted to catch me too. I was hoping Elizabeth got loose and was right behind me, but she wasn't.

Our mother didn't know. She called Elizabeth over and over again. Usually, Elizabeth would come, maybe a bit slower than I, but she would show up. This time, she did not come. For over an hour, Michelle called her. Then, thinking Elizabeth was playing and ignoring her, she became angry and said, "I give up! Stay out there!" If only she had known to run around to the alley, but could she have stopped those men?

The next morning, when Elizabeth was not at the back door, my mother looked astounded. "Where could she have gone?" she wondered. She asked me if I had seen Elizabeth. I could only close my eyes in sorrow and lower my head in grief. The look of horror in my eyes must have told her something terrible had happened, but she didn't really want to believe that. How could she?

Instead, my mother put up signs all over the neighborhood with a picture of Elizabeth taken on her birthday. She walked and searched all the streets and alleys, calling her name. She asked neighbors and even called the proper authorities to see if any dead bodies had been picked up, but there was no sign of her. Then, my mother cried and cried.

But perhaps the most horrifying of all was poor little Blossom. The day after Elizabeth disappeared, Blossom stood in the dining room window and screamed pitifully over and over again, "Mother! Mother! Mother!" It was almost too much to bear.

Eventually, my mother's quest to find Elizabeth led her to information that explained why almost every week in our neighborhood, there were signs posted about a missing pet. My mother learned there were people who went into neighborhoods around Washington, D.C. stealing people's pets to sell to labs for experiments. Some pets were even killed for their skins.

One lady told Mom of a refrigerator repairman who had gone into an animal mill in Virginia and had nearly fainted when he opened the refrigerator door. The refrigerator was full of skinned cats. This is a big business. Although there are laws against these things, these people are very powerful. Thus, many turn a blind eye to their actions. My mom tried to shield me from hearing these things, but I did hear them.

My Elizabeth was so beautiful with her white fur. The saddest thing was that her loving, trusting nature had led her into the hands of these terrible people. We were all in mourning for her sweet soul that had gone somewhere to hell on earth, and we could not do anything about it. When my mother finally realized what likely had happened to Elizabeth, she asked me again:

"Sabrina, what happened to Elizabeth? What did you see?"

Each time she asked, I closed my eyes and turned my head away in sorrow. The pain of what had happened to my daughter broke my heart. Even if I knew the words to describe what I had seen, I don't think I could ever bear to say them.

After this, we cats were not allowed to go outside unsupervised, and Mom gave Blossom and I collars with tags to wear. Of course, I would only sit on the back fence or the roof of the short building behind us. I never ventured on the ground back there or even in the front yard. No, I would be safe. Blossom was too afraid to go out at all.

During the weeks that followed Elizabeth's disappearance, my mother continued to talk to various people about her. One day, when Mom was feeling more brave than usual, she started calling labs to see if they might have bought a cat that looked like Elizabeth or knew of any labs that might be using stolen pets. A person at one of these labs told her they had heard something about the sale of pets from one of their associates. It involved some very powerful organizations, and the information led Mom to believe she might still be able to find our girl alive and get her back.

This hope and the memory of Elizabeth's sweet faith in the goodness of people led my mother to go places she should not have gone, even risking her own safety to do so. She told me she could picture Elizabeth sitting in a cage, waiting for her, and if there was anything at all she could do to get her back, she had to do it. She always believed that if she tried hard enough, she might succeed. We were her children, and there was nothing she would not do for us.

My mother tried all she could, but in this case, it was just too difficult. One Congressperson, who shall remain nameless, wanted my mother to carry a camera that looked like a briefcase in order to investigate some of the things these people were doing. I guess there had been other complaints, and there was talk of a hearing on Capitol Hill about this.

"Imagine that, Sabrina!" my mother said.

Well, Michelle was very adventurous, but not quite that adventurous. And unfortunately, those who had first-hand information were too afraid to come forth.

Finally, one of Mom's friends came over to visit. She had worked on Capitol Hill with Mom. In fact, the previous year this lady had adopted two of Elizabeth's children.

"I don't know if I want to talk to you anymore," the woman told her. "I'm afraid. You don't know what you are dealing with. You can't mess with these people. They have a lot of power and government connections. Your life is in danger. Don't think it's not."

Well, my mother began to get very nervous. To keep her spirits up, she kept picturing a movie about the search for Elizabeth, starring Whoopi Goldberg, á la *Jumpin' Jack Flash,* as her. But in the end, trying to find our dear Elizabeth was like trying to find a needle in a haystack (as those humans say). With great sorrow and many tears, my mother finally resigned herself to the truth, which I already knew.

Oddly enough, after this, notices for missing pets—which had appeared nearly every week for a year—stopped for a while.

Chapter 6
Our First Big Trip

With her mother gone, Blossom soon learned to live on her own. She certainly knew I was not going to be her mother, but we did live together in peace, deriving some small comfort in occupying the same space.

Then, at the end of this terrible year, Blossom and I took our first real trip—a three-week vacation in California. By now, Lindsay had moved next door, and that December all our roommates and everyone we knew was going away for Christmas. The only way our mother would be able to take her yearly trip and visit her family was to take us too.

First, Blossom and I had to go to the doctor for shots and health certificates. I didn't go for my shots every year; so, this was a novelty. Then, when the day came, we were each put in a cage and taken to Washington National Airport. We had never been in such a big place with so many people, and it was quite frightening.

Michelle insisted on taking us to the plane herself, rather than letting us go with the luggage, which I'm told is the usual way for pets. Sitting inside our cages, which were piled on a luggage cart, we went through a place with machines and lots of people opening suitcases. Then, we rode down a long walkway where we saw lots of legs. Finally, we were taken down a steep ramp and felt ourselves being handed over to some people who sat us on the ground outside. After that, we were put on a machine that pulled us up in the air, and someone put us in a big, dark area with lots of luggage. We didn't see any other animals there, only suitcases.

After a while, the doors closed and something made a slight clicking sound. This was followed by the sound of a huge rushing wind. Blossom and I had no idea what was going on, and we stood anxiously in our cages, uncertain of what to do or what to expect next.

After the roaring, rushing sound had gone on for a while, we felt the room we were in begin to move. Suddenly, the most terrifying sound began. It was the loudest rumble—a huge noise, and the air was pressing down on us from all sides. Then, the room started slanting upwards. Blossom was so scared she began to scream as loud as she could. Our mother later said she could hear her inside the plane! Following all these things, something very strange happened to us. It was as if a force was taking over us and the building we were in. Eventually, things quieted down to a steady roaring hum. Now, there was nothing for us to do but lie down and wait.

We landed in Dallas/Fort Worth, Texas (my mom told me that later). At this place, we were taken out of the plane and placed in a little car that took us to another area, where they put us back into something that looked like the place we had just been. Unbeknownst to us, Mom was upstairs having a time of it. She had been warned to make sure we were on the plane before it took off. So, she was trying to get the flight attendant to tell her that we definitely were down there in the hold. She had heard terrible tales about animals being left behind or put on the wrong plane.

After we got out of all the noise and terror for the second time, Mom met us, put us on a luggage cart and loaded us into a car to go to West Covina. We were in California! When Blossom and I finally got out of our cages, we were so shaken by our experience, we crawled under the bed by the wall and stayed there together for the rest of the day and all of the night. We didn't even want to eat. That trip was the most terrifying experience we ever had, or would have.

At the Prefontaine home (the name of Michelle's mother), we stayed in a nice suite of rooms. They consisted of a bedroom, bathroom and dressing room. We were completely shut off from the rest of the house in these rooms. So, after a nice rest and plenty of quiet, we came out and began to enjoy our stay.

Later during our stay, we sometimes had the use of the living room, which was connected to our suite by an entrance hall. The living room was a nice space with comfortable furniture and a huge corner window with lots of sunshine and a view of the street. Standing just in front of this window was a fresh Christmas tree, which Blossom and I found most interesting. It smelled good.

In the room we shared with our mom, Michelle, there were two single beds. While our mom slept in the bed next to the door, I spent most of my time on the bed by the large picture window, as did Blossom. The sun came in that window during the afternoon. How I loved lying in that warm California sunshine!

While we were in California, Blossom and I both had a chance to see Elizabeth's other daughter, Polly. Of course, no one expected us to get along after all this time, and we didn't, though Blossom and Polly sniffed noses. Polly was very territorial and somewhat snooty about her new position as queen of the house. Since we had our own private suite where she never ventured, we didn't worry about it. We were simply guests on a visit.

Life was fairly peaceful for us in California, but after nearly three weeks of looking out the window, I began to think of a way to get out and enjoy it on my own. One night, I saw a way to make my escape. Michelle had opened the bathroom window, just a little to let the air in. The window didn't have a screen; so, I slipped out and went exploring around the property.

Down on the lawn, I met another cat, who happened to be passing by. This cat and I got into a horrible fight. Of course, I began screaming at the top of my lungs when he jumped me, and Mom came running out of the house, desperately calling me. It was so dark she couldn't see; she actually stumbled over me in the grass. After that, I had had enough. She got me inside and found I had a little wound from the scuffle, but I was okay. What an adventure! I got the reputation of being a fighter after that.

Now, two days after my escape, we were supposed to go back to Washington, D.C. However, the night before we were to leave, Blossom decided that it was her turn to go out, and somehow she did. This was rather odd, as she never went out. Once she was out, I think she got frightened by a dog and went over to a neighbor's yard. Mom didn't know where she was, and she couldn't get her back that night. Blossom wasn't back in the morning either, which meant that we weren't going back to Washington that day because we certainly wouldn't leave without her!

The next day, Michelle's brother, Matthew, said he had seen Blossom, but he couldn't catch her. That night, she finally got the courage to come back, and Mom scheduled our flight. Boy, was she in trouble! Well, Blossom threw our trip off by one day, which meant we had a whole series of new adventures.

$$\mathbf{5}$$

We were returning the way we came, which meant we were stopping in Dallas/Fort Worth to change planes. At least this time, Blossom and I knew what to expect, and when we took off, Blossom didn't cry as hard.

Once we arrived in Dallas/Fort Worth though, there seemed to be a problem. We sat in our cages in the second plane, waiting and waiting. We could smell a very strong odor. After what seemed a long time, some men came, took us off the plane and put us some place on the side to wait.

By then, it must have been about eight or nine o'clock at night. Blossom and I had been in our cages since early that morning and we were pretty hungry and thirsty. We were just waiting and waiting, thinking any moment something would happen.

Then, suddenly, a huge storm rolled in. There was wind, rain, lightening and thunder. It was crazy. So, the men put us on a little truck and drove us to a place where they put us in a room with luggage.

Inside the airport, the passengers were told they would be put up for the night in a hotel. Mom told the airline she had two cats. They said she could leave us in the airport until six or seven in the morning, when she would fly out or she could take us to a hotel. Well, if I know my mom, she wasn't leaving us in the airport. After waiting some time, I heard my name being called over the loudspeaker of the airport!

"Sabrina Russell! Sabrina Russell! Please come to the Customer Service Desk!"

There was a pause and then again, "Sabrina Russell, you are wanted immediately at the Customer Service Desk."

I thought, "What? How am I a supposed to come to the Customer Service Desk when I'm in this cage? Who's calling my name?"

Mom said later she was running there, laughing all the way!

"They were calling you all over the airport, Sabrina! They didn't know they were calling a cat!"

Well, we got on a bus, and you never saw such rain in your life. The sky was black when we arrived and black when we left. Mom, Blossom and I got a hotel room with a big bed and a big glass door to the outside. All night, Blossom and I got up and looked out through the glass door at the water streaming down and flooding the ground. The wind was blowing the rain against the window in sheets. We sure were glad to be inside, able to stretch our legs and eat. Luckily, Mom had put a can of food in each of our cages. She also was able to create a makeshift toilet box with newspaper. We never did mess up our cages.

So, we slept in the hotel in Fort Worth, Texas (the only time I was in Texas), and the next morning we were off to the airport. We had another long wait in the plane until the storm passed, but finally we took off and got back to Washington, D.C. and home safely.

"Of all the times I've traveled," Mom said, "this had to happen when Sabrina and Blossom were there!"

We sure were glad to get home. We had had enough adventures for a while.

Chapter 7
Crazy Roommates and Others

During all the years we lived in the house on "G" Street, we had many different kinds of people live with us.

Of course, in my first two years, my mother and I lived in the small room at the end of the long hallway. With only the bathroom next to us, it was very private and quiet there. Our little cubbyhole was just big enough to fit a single bed, bookshelf, small chest of drawers—and us.

After Dan moved out, we had a roommate named Rodney. Rodney came to Washington, D.C. from Canada to attend the famed Gallaudet University, a school for the deaf. He often had friends from school come to visit him. They would sit in the dining room and communicate in a very lively way, making signs with their hands and sometimes stomping the floor or banging on the table to get each other's attention. I didn't understand exactly what was going on, but they were always very animated and interesting, so I would sit with them when I could.

After a while, Mom decided she didn't want me to hang out with Rodney. She didn't think he understood how to treat a cat. As I've said before, she always demanded that I be treated with respect.

Sometime in the spring of 1989, the house that was connected to ours became vacant, and Lindsay decided he wanted to have his own place with just one friend, rather than living in a group house like ours.

At that time, knowing Lindsay had originally brought me into the house and considered me half his, my mom asked if he was going to take me.

I think she was a little fearful about his answer, but thankfully he said, "Oh, no. She can stay with you. I'll be right next door and I can always visit her."

When Lindsay moved out, Mom rented the front room to a fellow named David. He had come up to D.C. from Florida and was kind of uncertain about what he wanted to do. He thought maybe he'd like to be involved in politics. He liked to watch TV in the living room a lot, and when my mom was there, he told her about hurricanes and his mother's friend who wrote a book called *Beaches*.

At David's suggestion, my mom worked to make the house homier. First, she went out and bought a dining room table and four chairs. This turned out to be nice for us cats. We liked to sleep on those chairs when they were pushed under the table. She also bought a lamp for the living room. The shade had a nice, stiff edge that we used to rub our backs against.

In the bathroom, there was a change we cats hardly noticed, except for the improved odor. Mom and David stripped off the old, moldy wallpaper and the grimy shower curtain, which covered the wall. In their place, they put up pretty, striped wallpaper and new paint. These changes made the bathroom feel clean and nice.

After that, whenever my mom had free time, she began to strip the old paint off the woodwork and repaint it. With all these changes, the house started to feel much nicer; it really felt like home.

David, however, was impatient with life in D.C. and decided it wasn't what he wanted. By the time he left, Rodney had already moved out, and we had moved into the middle room, which was a larger and more comfortable space for us. There was one large disadvantage to this room; every time someone took a shower, we could hear the water running in our wall.

Another disadvantage was that the window, which faced the back yard, was between two walls, which limited our view and made the room somewhat dark. At least, I could still sit and look out. I think Blossom and I each startled someone at one time or another because our window was also right next to the bathroom window ("kitty corner," they call it). In fact, if the curtains were open, I could look right in and see anyone who was in there. It was very interesting.

After David left, my mom rented the front room to another guy from Florida, named "Paul." When Paul first moved in, he seemed to be really friendly, but, in truth, he wasn't so much. I remember at first he wanted a house that was going to be very clean. Then, he never washed his dishes. The pile in the sink got higher and higher. My mom washed some of his dishes, but as the days passed, she got mad and said she wasn't going to wash any more.

Finally, Paul's dishes were filling the sink and covering the counter. Mom took a few out and washed them, so we would have something to eat on. The rest of the dirty dishes, she put in a box and left under the kitchen table near our cat dishes. Boy, did they stink!

One day, Paul finally came in and he wasn't pleased. He did wash his dishes, though. Then, after a few months in the house, he said he wasn't happy living there and he left.

Meanwhile, our old bedroom was rented to a fellow who worked on political campaigns for congressmen, senators and even presidents. (My mother had to give me some help on this information, as I don't know anything about campaigns or what people did outside the house.) This fellow's name was Peter, and it seemed as if campaigning was his life. He left early in the morning and came home late at night. When he was home, he just went to his room and watched TV. He never cooked, and on the weekends he went to stay with his girlfriend. Sometimes I would see my mom and him talking in the hall, but I only went down there to peek in our old room and see what had happened to it.

About this time, Mom rented the front room to a guy from Tucson, Arizona, who seemed very nice and very smart. We'll call him "Jed." Jed was a writer, and his ambition was to work for a big newspaper. He was always up in his room typing. Sometimes, he would come downstairs, and he and my mom would have long, intense conversations.

The only thing about Jed that my mother didn't know was that he hated cats. Of course, he didn't tell her that when he was looking for a place to stay. No, that first day when we approached him during his interview, we jumped up on the arms of the big, gray chair where he was sitting, and he petted us and acted very friendly. Maybe he had not always hated cats, but in time, it seemed that way. After a while, when Mom was not around, he was a different person. He would do things to scare us and take his anger out on us. We were terrified.

For a long time, Mom suspected nothing, but in time she figured it out. One clue was that whenever we were sitting in the living room with her and we heard Jed coming up the stairs to the front door, we would run out of the room and hide. Blossom and I learned to avoid him; especially poor Blossom, who was already afraid of most people. Sometimes, when Blossom thought someone was after her, she would go into a corner and scream in terror. Jed's behavior toward her certainly didn't help.

Things with Jed finally came to a head about nine months after he moved in. A large, skinny cat with orange and white fur showed up in our backyard one day. He was very sweet, but deathly thin. It was obvious he had been living on the lam, scrounging in garbage cans for his survival. Now, he had nearly run out of hope, so he gave up his pride and started to approach anyone he thought might help him and give him some food.

My mom could tell immediately what his situation was and she began to leave water out for him, as well as some of our food. He was a sweet boy. I would sometimes see him outside in the yard, lounging in the sun, happy that at last someone had given him something to eat. At this point, he had little energy to keep running, and our courtyard seemed to be a safe haven.

Felix

In happiness, each morning and sometimes in the afternoon, he would hop up on the windowsill and look in to see if he could catch Mom's attention. He was in this position one day, when Jed walked in and saw him.

Mom was preparing our food, and Jed got mad. He said he didn't like that cat out there and she was not to feed him. I don't know what Mom thought, but she ignored him. Her only concern was with the cat, whom she had named Felix, because of his good nature. She was still grieving Elizabeth, and Felix seemed like a blessing. He was an angel soul whom she could help.

Shortly, after Jed said what he did, Felix disappeared for several days. Mom didn't say anything, but she was worried that Jed had done something to frighten him away. She even went looking for Felix, knowing he had no home and was in desperate need of food.

Two days later, Felix showed up, very weak and tired. It was obvious that he had been frightened away and had tried in vain to find another place. Now, he was on his last legs, in desperate need of shelter, food and rest.

That night, Mom snuck him up to our room. We really didn't mind him being there, for after he ate, he curled up, purring happily and went to sleep. At last, he could rest and not fear for his life.

The next morning, Mom took him downstairs and was feeding him when Jed walked into the room. Seeing Felix in the kitchen eating, Jed went into a rage. We cats ran into the dining room, scared to death of his yells. He ran toward Felix, who by then was in front of the door, trying desperately to get out, and began kicking at him and roaring at the top of his voice.

"I told you not to let that dirty, stinking cat in here. He's full of disease. I will kill that damn cat if I ever see him again . . ."

My mom was behind Jed, screaming for him to stop, but he continued to try to kick the cat, yelling curses at it. At that point, Blossom had hidden under the desk in the dining room, but I was peering around the corner, my hair on end, afraid for our mom.

Mom was screaming and yelling, "Don't hurt that cat! How dare you hurt him! You are not the only one who lives in this house!"

Then, in a fury to stop Jed, Mom hauled off and hit him. She wanted to take the attention off Felix, onto herself. It was horrifying. Jed's shock at being hit gave her enough time to open the door and let Felix out.

At this point, Lindsay came running through the back door. He looked scared to death and ready to fight. I think the whole neighborhood must have heard Jed's horrible yells and Mom's screams.

"Michelle, are you all right? I was going to call the police," he said, giving Jed a look.

Mom told him she was okay. Her real concern was about Felix. Jed went off to his room and then to work, while Mom went out to find Felix. She knew she must find him a safe haven, so she took him to Jane's Veterinary to board, while she tried to find him a home.

During the time Felix was at the vet, he tested positive for Feline Leukemia. This meant he could not live with us because we might also become infected. It also meant it would be harder to get him a home. However, a short time after putting up several signs on the Capitol Hill Congressional bulletin board, a man called who was staying in D.C. and was lonely for the company of a cat.

This man took Felix into his home and said he would pay for him to go to a natural healing vet who had had success in stabilizing Feline Leukemia. Mom went with the man to take Felix to the vet. After examining him, the vet thought Felix's condition was not too grave. He gave Felix all kinds of vitamins and special foods to eat. Later, I heard my mom talking about this, and she actually went to visit Felix in his new home, only a few blocks from us. He had a very good life for a while. Then one day, the man let him out on the deck to sun himself. Felix jumped off, and was never seen again.

About three months after this terrible event, Jed moved. I cannot tell you how relieved Blossom and I were. Prior to this event, our mother had enjoyed Jed's company, but she could never have imagined how much that man frightened us.

ʒ

Following the uncertainties of all these men coming and going, Mom decided to let a nice, young girl named Crystal come to live with us. Crystal was only seventeen years old, which was a concern, but her references were excellent and, most importantly, she really loved cats, so Mom accepted her as our next housemate.

Crystal was from Minnesota. Her parents died when she was small, and her aunt and uncle raised her. She had come to Virginia to work as a nanny. Now, she was going to attend school in order to get a better job.

Crystal was very sweet, and we were glad to be around her. Even Blossom had no reason to fear her. After Crystal moved in, the two of us started spending more time in the living room.

Around this time, Peter, the political campaign guy, moved out, and Mom decided to rent to another girl who needed a place. This girl had been living with her grandmother and wanted to get out on her own. We will call her "Mandy."

Mandy was a big girl, tall and heavy with dark hair. She had a friendly but crying kind of voice. She liked to eat, and though Mom said, "No smokers," I could smell cigarette smoke on her. She was quite friendly to us cats when she came for her interview, but she was also fast talking and very nervous, which didn't give me good vibes. Maybe, I could have told my mom this girl was not such a great choice for a housemate, but who would listen to me?

Until you live with someone, you never really know what they're like. Not long after she moved in, Mandy had the entire floor of our former room piled twice my height with papers and junk. Mom told me to stay out of there because I kept going down the hall to look at it. I think Mandy would have liked me to stay with her, but staying out of that room was no problem for me. To be honest, I was a little afraid of the girl. She walked heavy and talked loud. Furthermore, she smoked in that room piled high with paper. She also had a jar that she spat in after smoking, and it stank.

My mom tried to be friendly to Mandy because she felt kind of sorry for her. Mandy lost her mother when she was very young and she had a lot of issues. She would come home from work nearly every day with a complaint about someone or a hurt they had done her. Then, she would buy a cake and eat the whole thing. She told to Mom, "But it says 'fat-free,' I don't know why I'm gaining weight."

Mom insisted that Mandy clean her room and not smoke in the house. We could smell the smoke coming down the hallway. Mandy denied that she was smoking. She said she had quit. Then, there was an entirely different matter.

Mom found out that Mandy didn't like black people. She was living in our house, and Crystal and Mom had many black friends. In fact, Crystal's boyfriend was black. Mandy's prejudice really irritated Mom. I heard Mandy say nasty things about every black person she saw. She was real snooty about that, but she didn't have anything to be snooty about.

Look at us cats. We are black and white and all mixed colors. Does that make one cat better than another? I don't think so. You might like a white cat or an orange cat or a black cat, but that's a matter of personal preference and attraction. One is no better than the other.

Anyway, it seems Mandy voiced some of her nasty opinions one day when she and Mom were out in public. That really got Mom mad. Mandy said she wanted to get away from black people, and Mom asked her, "So, if you don't like black people, why are you living in Washington, D.C.?" (D.C. was known for being 80% black.)

Mom came home really angry at Mandy's hurtful attitude, and Mandy was angry as well. After that, they were no longer on speaking terms. Mom wondered how she ended up with such a prejudiced person living in her house.

By this time, Mom had left her job on Capitol Hill and was working in various offices during the day. On the weekends, she took singing lessons. Then, she began trying out for shows. At night, she stayed in our room practicing her vocal lessons and singing songs for us. Blossom and I really enjoyed that a lot.

In the spring, Mom got a part in a show called *My Fair Lady,* and many evenings she was out at rehearsal. When she was home, she spent most of her free time in the bedroom with us. That way, she didn't have to deal with company or seeing Mandy in one of her bad moods. There was almost nothing more irritating in the world to Mom than a person who insisted on being hurt and angry at the world.

Late one night, Mom, Blossom, and I were sitting quietly in our room when we heard Mandy stomping up the stairs and then coming down the hall toward her room. As she passed our door, she said something like, "She thinks she can fool me. Well, I'll show her."

When Mandy got to the end of the hall, she went into her room and slammed the door. A minute later, she came out again and started back down the hall toward our door. We could hear her talking about "Michelle." I looked at my mom, and she looked at me. Then we both looked at the door. Was she going to come in our room? It was pretty tense for a few moments.

This happened several times over the next week. Mandy would come walking real heavy down the hall. Then, as she neared our door everything stopped, and we would look at one another. Mandy was saying, "She thinks she's so smart. I'll show her."

Finally, my mom started putting a chair in front of the door for protection. Mandy never did try to come into our room, but we were pretty scared. We both thought she was a little nuts.

Now, I'll tell you a secret about something that happened with Crystal. Every day, Crystal had to get up at five in the morning to go to school. Mandy usually got up about six, and my mom seldom got up before eight. This way, Mom avoided seeing anyone but us cats in the morning, which was exactly the way she liked it.

Anyway, on this particular morning I happened to be downstairs when Crystal came down to get her breakfast before she left for school. As she turned the corner, there was Mandy standing in the middle of the kitchen stark naked and about as furry as I am. She was blow-drying her hair, and she had all the lights on because it was still dark outside. There were no curtains on the windows either.

Crystal was so shocked; she didn't know what to say.

"Humpf," said Mandy, really loud. She was mad that Crystal had come into the kitchen, but what was she doing in the kitchen naked? My mom never did anything like that.

Crystal grabbed her food and left, saying, "Well, I have to get my food for school. I don't have money to buy any."

Later, Crystal tried to apologize, but Mandy continued to be angry with her. As usual, I stayed out of it. I just observed everything in my usual quiet cat way, and then I disappeared! Oh, the things we cats see!

Now, Mandy really liked cats, and she'd had a hard life. She had been living with her grandmother, but her grandmother was an irritating woman. She'd moved in with us to try to make a new start. Then, like most people, she didn't solve the problems in herself, but blamed them on everyone else. So, the new location didn't help things much.

In the beginning, Mandy talked to me a lot and petted me. I think she was looking for love. When Blossom let her, she'd even pet Blossom. But no one could really help Mandy because she had not healed her own hurt inside. Instead, she always thought other people were hurting her. It was a no-win situation.

Chapter 8
Oh, No! More Kittens!

Yes, for some crazy, unknown reason, my mother brought eight mother-less kittens into our home! The way it happened was this:

Crystal's boyfriend, whom we shall call "Lou," was living in a boarding house in a very bad area of Washington, D.C. (around 14th Street NW). The owner of the house rented rooms to several people, and he also had a cat that was very pregnant. About two or three days after this cat gave birth, a crazy man killed it, leaving her eight kittens orphaned.

Crystal came into the living room the day after this happened and told my mother the story, asking what she could do to save them. She told my mom, "Michelle, the owner has them in a box on the porch, and I'm afraid some animal will come and eat them. Not only that, but he put a saucer with cold milk in the center of the box and said, 'if they are hungry, they will eat.' Their eyes are not even open yet!"

"That milk will kill them!" my mother said. "It will stop up their insides. Baby cats can't digest cow's milk. I know this from experience."

Then, she thought about it and asked, "Does the owner really want these kittens?"

"Yes, he says he's going to sell them," said Crystal.

"I'll tell you what we should do," said Mom, "Get a cab, go over to the house, get that box of kittens and bring them here. We'll take care of them."

Crystal made an excited little jump and smiled. "Oh, I was hoping you'd say that!"

Of course, knowing my mother, she wanted to rescue them. She gave Crystal some money for the cab and all was set. Crystal got the kittens without the owner catching her, and Mom got instructions from Jane's Veterinary for their care. She needed powdered queen's milk or cat milk, two doll bottles and baby vitamins.

At least she knew not to bother me with them. I had no interest in kittens! The surprise was she thought that Blossom might want to take care of them, just as she had taken care of her mother's kittens. But Blossom said, "No way!" When the kittens arrived, she took one look at them, hissed, and walked out of the room.

The babies' eyes were still closed, and they were so tiny, they looked like mice. When Crystal brought them into our house, they had not eaten in a day and they were all crying. Crystal and my mom sat down with the doll bottles and fed them. When they finished feeding one, they started over

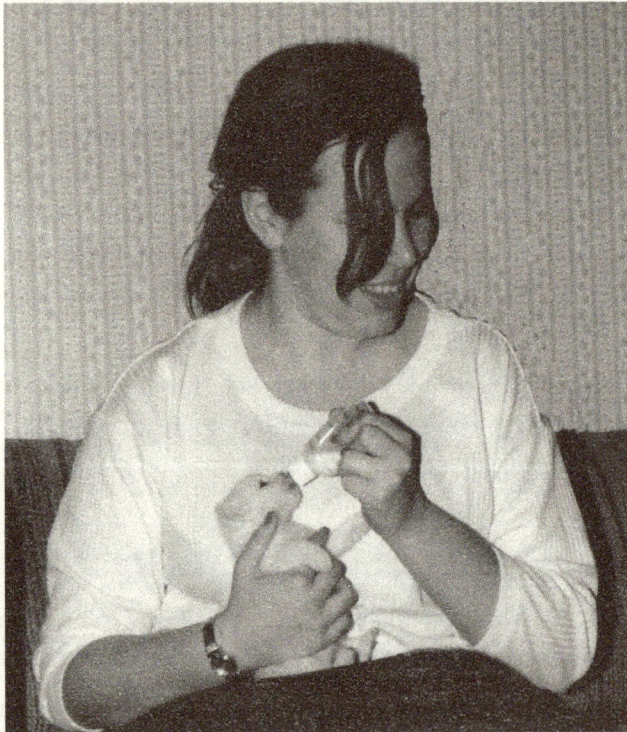

Crystal feeding a baby kitten

again with the next one. It took a while to feed eight kittens. In the beginning, each one got about half a bottle. The kittens all did very well.

The babies were supposed to be fed every four to six hours, and with their schedules, Mom and Crystal were able to do this. Crystal would feed them at four or five in the morning, and Mom would feed them between eight and nine. Then, Crystal fed them again at one in the afternoon. At five o'clock, Mom and Crystal fed them together. After that, Crystal fed them between nine and ten o'clock, before she went to bed, and Mom fed them again at one in the morning, after she got home from working in the show. You see, it was an around-the-clock operation.

When the kittens were being fed, it was rather noisy in the living room. With only one or two people to feed them, the others would have to wait, and the ones that were waiting were always screaming for their turn. Once they had their share, and the bottle was taken away, they would scream again for more. This schedule went on for three or four weeks. At least in the beginning, when they weren't eating, the babies were sleeping. Thank goodness!

After using queen's milk for a couple of weeks, Mom found it was too expensive and started mixing some watered down cow's milk, along with baby vitamins, into the formula. This started the kittens pooping.

Mom had to learn to do all the things that mother cats do with their tongues. She had to get a wet cloth and wipe kittens' tummies in one direction to make them pee and then wash it off. When the kittens started pooping, she had to wash their dirty behinds in a teacup, while they cried. Then, she had to rub all the parts of their tiny bodies to give them love and make them grow. See all the things we mother cats do!

Mostly, the kittens lived downstairs in a box in the living room or dining room where the girls could get to them. Once in a while, I would peek in on them and then give them a hiss. When Mom went to work, she locked them in her room, and Blossom and I stayed downstairs.

I was always happy to have quiet time with my mom, but as you can see, there wasn't much of it. Most of the time she was around, I was sitting on the back of the couch or the chair, just observing what was going on.

Eight kittens at four weeks

Around the time Mom was having trouble with Mandy, the kittens had reached the stage where they were able to get out of the box and run around. To keep them safe, Mom put them in the kitchen with a suitcase across the doorway, to prevent them from running into the rest of the house.

The kittens had no trouble learning to use the toilet box, but they had a terrible time learning to eat on their own. They were always looking up for a bottle. They'd run right through their saucer of milk and never seem to notice that there was milk in it.

Finally, Mom's friend, Alice, suggested giving the babies bread soaked in milk. In this way, the kittens learned to suck the milk out of the bread. From there, they learned to eat. All in all, it took about three weeks for them to catch on to the regular process of eating. (I sniffed at that bread with milk and didn't want it.) But once they learned to eat, those eight kittens were soon gobbling everything up like crazy and running all over the house.

The kittens were all very little and very fast, and I remember Mom was afraid that Mandy, who walked so heavy and always seemed to be off in another world, might step on one. She had already stepped on my foot once and made me cry. She just was not very aware of things.

Once the kittens started playing, Blossom became fascinated with them and decided she might want to play too. At night, she would lick their heads a little bit. She wasn't too involved, but she was curious about them and wanted to have some fun. After all, she was still pretty young herself.

The largest and smallest kittens in the group were both striped tabbies with white paws. The tiniest one, a female, Mom named "Titi" (Tee-tee). There was also a black and white kitten. The rest were all white.

Because the kittens had been raised by human hands, Mom said they were special, and, when it was time for them to leave, she was very particular about where each kitten went. Two kittens were adopted by an actress and moved to Arizona, one went to our neighbor's rich friend, and another two were taken by two women who were neighbors. They were going to name the kittens after their mothers who had passed on.

In the whole group, there were only two boys. One, Titi's twin, was the biggest kitten, a tabby with white feet and a white chest. The other was the black kitten, also with white feet and chest. Crystal wanted to keep one of the boy kittens, and decided on the biggest one, the tabby boy. She named him "Theo."

So finally, after many months, there were only three cats left in the house: Blossom, me, and Crystal's kitten, Theo. There had been so much life going on in our house, it now seemed amazingly quiet, but that was how I liked it.

A few months later, Mom decided that no matter what, Mandy had to move. The problem was more than her attitude toward Mom; she was now taking things out on Crystal as well. And despite Mom's demands that she clean her room, she never had. Mom was terribly worried that one night, with the condition of her room and her smoking, she would set the house on fire.

Mom decided the best and easiest way to handle the situation was to tell Mandy that she and Crystal were moving, and the landlady wanted the house back. In this way, there would be no hurt feelings or arguments. After Mom told Mandy she was moving, Mom started packing up her books and piling boxes in the dining room. Mandy kept saying, "I don't know where I will go. I can't go back to my grandmother's. That woman drives me crazy!"

At the end of the month, having no other options, Mandy moved back to her grandmother's house with all her boxes and bags of junk. What a relief!

Mom told Mandy that she had to stay another week or so to clean the house, but after Mandy was gone, Crystal's boyfriend, Lou, moved in. Although Lou was spending most of his time with Crystal, he agreed to rent the back room.

One day, a few weeks later, the phone rang. When Mom answered, it was Mandy. She had called to check on the house, and now she knew Mom and Crystal were still there. I don't know what Mom told her, but Mandy wasn't very happy about it.

For a while, things worked out with Lou, but he was used to being the king of his own domain. He didn't really like us cats all that much either. He spanked Blossom and me, which was something Mom was not happy about. She didn't want anyone laying a hand on us. Besides, you can't train a cat by spanking them, that's for sure. We just sneak and do what we want anyway! Ha! All it does is ruin our disposition. With Mom, we generally behaved by being spoken to. At least, I did.

One day, Mom came home, and Lou was spanking Theo very hard with his big hand. Lou said he had told Theo to get down from the counter and he had gotten up there again. Mom was very uncomfortable with this and told him not to hit Theo again. He was a baby and he would learn in time.

Lou soon decided to move out. After that, we knew that Crystal might not be far behind, but she wasn't ready to move quite yet. First, she had to finish school.

When Crystal was finally ready to move, she said she would let Theo stay with us until she got settled. Mom was glad. By now, she had grown very attached to Theo and could not imagine him not being with us. Whenever she watched TV in the living room, she would sit in the big gray chair, with him snuggled up in her arms. She said he was like a teddy bear, and she couldn't help falling in love with him. She never did know how jealous I was.

Meanwhile, Crystal kept delaying when she was going to take Theo to live with her. Every time my mom thought about Theo leaving, she would sit there with tears coming down her cheeks.

Theo had always seen Crystal as his second Mommy, but after she moved away, even though she came to see him, she was sort of out of his life. Whenever she came to visit, he acted as if she had deserted him and was not very friendly to her. I think he also realized she was planning to take him away from the place he considered home, as well as Mom and Blossom— his family. Since the time Crystal moved, Blossom and Theo had become very attached to one another. Theo loved her, and she loved him.

Finally one day, Crystal came to get Theo. Prior to this, I think Mom had mentioned to her that she really loved Theo and if he ever needed a home, he was welcome to come back. When Crystal came in the door that day, the first thing she noticed was that Theo was not happy to see her. Then, she witnessed how he and Blossom were together. She said to Mom, "I think, if

Theo

it's alright with you, I should leave Theo here. I see how much he and Blossom love one another, and I can't part them."

Crystal really had a good heart.

So, that is how it was. We were now three, and like it or not, we would be three for the next eleven years.

Chapter 9
Neighbors, Roommates & Michelle

In the last chapters, I have described our lives in Washington, D.C. but until now I have not mentioned our neighbors or anything about being in our nation's capital.

The meaning of our capital was far too big for me to comprehend, but I did take note when Socks Clinton moved into the White House. We had his framed picture and paw print hanging on our dining room wall. Mom would often point it out to us. All I can say about that is, "After all those dogs, it was about time we had a cat in the White House!"

Next door to our house was a charming, little, white house. It was probably the oldest home on our street. Bob and Suzanne lived there with their dog. They had a lovely garden, and every once in a while, I would sneak over there to smell the flowers.

On the other side of our home was the house where Lindsay moved. He and his friend, Brian, planted a garden and made it very pretty. Beyond that was a row of modern town houses where some children lived. Sometimes, I would venture down there, but not often.

In the early '90s, Lindsay and Brian moved away, and a woman with two cats moved next door. As a treat for her cats, she planted a big pot of catnip in the backyard. Whenever I went out, that was the first place I headed. It was neat.

About the same time our new neighbor moved in, Crystal moved out, and Mom decided that it was time for us to move to the big room up front, where we would have lots of space, a big closet and two large windows. My escape from the other cats was that I now had my own window, and Blossom and Theo had theirs. Unfortunately, the views and sounds in this front room were not always pleasant: cars speeded up Sixth Street, horns honked, people fought and women screamed for help. Sometimes, we even heard pops, which Mom thought might be gunshots. It could be quite nerve-wracking, and Mom didn't always like us sitting in those windows.

After Lou moved out, the back room was rented to a nice man from Pennsylvania named Steve. He worked on Capitol Hill. We didn't see him too much, except on weekends. The man who moved into our old room, the middle room, was from a foreign country and unlike anyone we had ever lived with before.

Barthosa was from Nigeria, and he spoke with an accent. He was black, very, very, tall and very thin. He was a happy man, always laughing and soon had many friends. Most of them were women who would come to our house and gather around him, talking and laughing for an entire evening.

The other unusual thing about Barthosa was that he was an artist. I would sit on the cabinet in the kitchen window and watch him at work in the back yard. He would take big pieces of wood and carve them. Then, he would hold something with fire coming out of it and burn the wood pieces black. It smelled strange, but it was fascinating. Barthosa said his work was a unique art form from Nigeria, and he got some public attention for this.

When our new neighbor, whom we shall call "May," moved in, Mom welcomed her warmly. We were a close neighborhood where people knew one other and said "hello" on the street. In the spring, Mom had a big dinner party with Barthosa and her friends. She also invited May and one of May's friends to come as well. It was a very nice affair. In those days, my mom enjoyed cooking and using her new dining room table.

Not long after this lovely dinner party, my mom learned that May was planning to have the grand, old pear tree in the back yard cut down. Mom was horrified and called the landlady, who told her she had promised to let May cut it down and she couldn't go back on her word. Even though we had lived there for over six years, we had no say.

Our courtyard with the old pear tree, just about to bloom. Blossom can be seen walking along the fence.

Mom called May to try and convince her to change her mind. She told her the tree was the most beautiful thing in the yard. She said it gave the squirrels something to eat. Later, I heard Mom repeat May's response many times. May's comment was, "Well, the squirrel's can go get a job and buy their own food." Imagine that!

No matter what Mom said in favor of keeping the tree, May would not budge. Mom even pointed out that the tree's trunk was actually on our side of the yard, but May wasn't listening.

When our housemate, Steve, learned of her plan to cut down the old tree, he became very angry. He was not around a lot, but on the weekends, the pear tree was the one thing he could look at out the window of his small room and enjoy. Otherwise, there was nothing but bricks, fences and back porches! In addition, during the summer, the tree made the back of the house much cooler.

Mom told Steve she was trying to stop plans to cut down our beautiful tree, which was just about to burst into bloom. When Mom told Steve that May was "horrified" because she sometimes hung her clothes to dry from the pear tree's branches, he said, "If she cuts that tree down, I am going to put up a clothesline and hang out underwear that NEVER comes down."

Meanwhile, the entire neighborhood was abuzz with the news of May's plans. They had looked upon this tree's beauty for years and were up in arms against its destruction. Neighbors were calling the landlady, but to no avail.

One weekend, Blossom, Mom and I were out enjoying the beauty of this old tree, full of glorious, white blossoms, and a few days later, it was gone. It felt as if someone had died.

True to his word, the next week, Steve had three lines of shorts and socks hanging in the backyard. One year after destroying this beautiful, old tree, May moved out.

❧

Although I was now getting close to an age that would be considered a "senior" in the cat world, I was active and healthy. Once in a while, I even played with my toys.

Theo was a grown cat now, and I didn't want to be anywhere near him. Consequently, Mom began to feed me on top of the file cabinet in the kitchen, away from the other two. At night, I slept on the inside top corner of Mom's bed, on a pillow made just for me, while Blossom and Theo slept together at the foot of the bed. In this way, our lives were fairly peaceful. Blossom and Theo had their lives, and I had mine.

I must say my granddaughter, Blossom, had a neat trick that she did. It was chasing her tail—something I never did. Blossom could go round and round and round and round without stopping. It was like a dance, and I enjoyed watching her.

During this time, my mom began working at the John F. Kennedy Center for the Performing Arts. She loved it. She brought home music from *Les Miserables*, *The Phantom of the Opera* and various singers, and we would all listen to it in our room. We really enjoyed that. She was also working hard on her singing with a vocal coach and began doing a few one-woman shows. We had the privilege of watching the rehearsals for these shows at home.

It seemed as if Mom was always falling in love and being disappointed. I was always there for her during these episodes, and she knew it. I would try to comfort her when she cried. Even Blossom, who was still afraid to have Mom approach her, came to her and licked the tears off her cheeks.

Among the great trials I witnessed my mom experience during this time was the passing of her best friend, Robin. Although I had never met Robin, I saw the deep grief Mom felt at the loss of her friend. There was little I could do but be there with her. Meanwhile, no one really knew all I felt.

Chapter 10
Our Brave New York Adventure

L ife seemed to be going along fine for us, but Mom was restless. She had gone through some things that made her very unhappy, and after being in another show, during which time we hardly ever saw her, I knew she was thinking about making other plans. I just didn't know what they were.

One day, shortly after a new roommate moved in, my mother, Michelle, packed up a lot of things and told us we were going on a trip. I assumed it would be much like the other trip we had taken, traveling to a very nice place where we could all lounge around and enjoy ourselves. This was not to be the case.

One cold evening in November, a young man arrived with a small car. He packed us (in our cages) in the back seat of the car and then surrounded us on three sides with my mother's belongings. We were packed in tight. Mom climbed in, and off we went into the dark night.

That cold night, it seemed a very long ride, and Blossom cried. Finally, we arrived somewhere, and my mom took us into this building with a long hallway that stunk. After speaking to a man at the desk, Mom carried us through a door into two rooms. One room contained a bed, television and dresser. The other room was small and empty with only a window and a very dirty carpet. You could tell other animals had been there before us.

So there we were. "This is it?" I asked myself. "This is what our big trip was about?" I know my mom was not feeling great, but she made do by putting our clean sheets and comforter on the bed. After that, she set up our toilet box in the small dirty room. We settled ourselves on the bed. Only when it became absolutely necessary, did we get up to drink the water our mother had placed on the floor for us. There was some food there as well, which we cats all shared. Although I considered Blossom and Theo my enemies, I now realized that we three were in this together and we needed one another.

In the morning, the lonely yowling of a hungry cat awakened us. Looking out the window next to the bed, I could see a large barren piece of land surrounded on all sides by tall buildings. There was no color here; everything was gray. There was not a tree or a blade of grass of any kind—only rocks and the garbage people had apparently thrown out of the windows from the surrounding buildings. All that and the lonely cat.

During the day, my mom went out to look for work. Sometimes in the evenings, she was out working on her show; the show that had been her reason for coming here. She planned to perform the show she had been doing in Washington, D.C. At least, Mom had an escape from this terrible place. We were stuck there, in the dirt, the smell, and the gray depression.

I will never forget the day I woke up to my mother's scream. Theo had caught a little mouse, which had come through a hole in the floor, and he was throwing it through the air. My mom didn't want him to kill it or eat it; so, she took it from him in a paper and tried to stuff the half-dead mouse back down through the hole in the floor.

A little while later, there was a knock at the door. It was the neighbor girl, who had gotten to be a little friendly with Mom. "Is everything okay?" she asked.

"Oh, yes," said my mom, "It was just the mouse Theo caught."

"I thought maybe there were mice here," the girl responded, "I hear them running in the walls at night."

Every day our room seemed to get colder. To keep warm, we three cats put aside our differences and huddled together in a lump under the blankets. This was how Mom found us when she came back from work in the evening.

The air in the room was icy, not only because there was not enough heat, but because the windowpanes were broken and pieces of glass were missing.

The cold, cold wind that blew off the nearby Hudson River was also blowing in our room. We were not very happy, but we trusted our mom to take care of us. So, we hung together.

My mother said she was sorry. She knew that either we had to find another place very soon, or else go back to Washington, D.C. I was all for returning to my clean, safe home in D.C. but I knew my mom wanted to stay on in New York because she wanted to sing.

Meanwhile, a very, kind man lent us his heater for the night. Oh, we were so happy. We came out from under the covers for that. The next day, Mom bought blankets, nails and a hammer. She actually hammered blankets over the windows. On top of the blankets, she put plastic. It made the room dark, but at least it was warm. When the wind blew, we could see the blankets and plastic moving, but we were protected from the cold wind. Soon after that, Mom bought us our own heater. Still, the room was dark and gloomy, and we didn't feel safe being there.

One reason for our feeling of insecurity was the man next door. We were living next to a crazy, old man. He was so dirty we could actually smell his greasiness through the wall. All night, every night, he played his television loudly and yelled curses. One night, when Mom went out to use the dirty, shared bathroom in the hall, the man came out of his room, and seeing her, let out a stream of fowl language such as she had never heard. It was awful.

After we had lived in these rooms for several weeks, everyone in the building received a notice that they were going to have to move. The city wanted to use the motel to house people with AIDS. My mom said the poor AIDS patients would die from the cold in that place. One man there told her, "Oh this place is nice. The other place I lived had pools of blood on the hallway floor, where people got stabbed."

The night Mom got that notice, she stood on line with a lot of other residents, waiting to use the pay phone in the hall. There were no cell phones back then. When her turn came, she spoke to her mother and other friends. Then, she came back to our room, and said, "If God wants us to stay, we'll get another place in a week. Otherwise, we'll go home."

I was still hoping we would go home, but the following week, Mom found a place. So after nearly a month in this hell hole, we were loaded up in our cages along with everything else, put in a cab, and off we went.

It was only a few blocks to our new place. From the cab, we were taken into a large, old building with a big, bright entry hall and a wide, curving staircase. Some guy with long hair and glasses came down and helped carry us up five flights of stairs, to a warm, wood-floored apartment. It smelled clean, and that was a relief!

We were immediately taken into a medium-sized room with a large bed, dresser and closet. There was a window as well, though the view was only of another building. The buildings were very close; so, there was not much light. Still, the place felt safe.

As soon as I came out of the cage and sat on the bed, I saw two curly-headed dogs peeking through the door. I arched my back and hissed at them, just to let them know I was ready to attack.

"Come now," said the long-haired man to the dogs, and they ran away.

"Okay," I thought and settled myself on a pillow. All in all, so far, this place seemed pretty good, especially after the last one. Most importantly, it was warm and peaceful.

I will describe the new apartment. You came in the front door. To the right was a large, white kitchen with a table and a nice window. Across from this, on the other side of the hall, was a bathroom. The next-door down from the kitchen was our room. The room just after ours was our roommate, Richard's room. Then, at the end of the long, narrow hallway there was a bright, sunny living room with big windows that looked down on a street known as Amsterdam Avenue. The walls were yellow, but so old the paint was falling from the ceiling onto the floor. There was a TV in this room, but my mom rarely took us there, or even went there herself. Just off this room, was another bedroom where an actor lived.

According to my mom, a friend in Washington, D.C. had arranged for her to make some Equity (the theatre union for actors) connections, and that was how she got this apartment. She was hoping the Equity connection meant the place was safe and inhabited by respectable people. Richard was a theatrical agent, and Oliver was a classically-trained African-American actor. Although my mom had not yet met Oliver and had been worried about him not getting along with us, he was the person who became our very best, kind and trusted friend.

Once we were securely settled in the new apartment, my mom went to work. She was lucky to get full-time work for a while. After Christmas, she decided to go back to D.C. to check on our house. She left Blossom and Theo for Richard to take care of during the two days she was gone. Richard called Blossom a "glamour girl, the Lana Turner of cats."

Mom didn't want to leave me alone with Theo and Blossom; so, she took me to stay with her friend, Susan. I really wanted to go D.C. with her, but she told me she was traveling by bus, and I wouldn't be allowed on the bus.

Susan's apartment was okay. There were two nice windows, lots of plants, and plenty of air and light. Susan was very solicitous to me, but I was not happy without my mom. Later, she told Mom that while I was there, all I did was complain.

After the New Year, things came to a head. Originally, the plan had been for us to stay in New York about three months. Then, Mom found out she would not be allowed to do the show she had originally planned for legal reasons; so, she had to create a new show. That was going to take longer.

Meanwhile, along with working full-time in the day, she started attending singing classes on the weekends, and sometimes rehearsals at night. When she came home, she would lie on the bed with us and read. It was a very quiet life for us, but as I said, at least we were safe and warm. We also heard our mom spending time in the kitchen, talking to Richard and Oliver.

As secure as we were, after a short time, Mom began to feel uncomfortable about this place too. I did as well. I would sleep on my mom's inside pillow against the wall, next to her head and, as usual, Theo and Blossom would sleep together at the foot of the bed.

In the middle of the night, we were often awakened by the sound of heavy feet in the hall. Following this, we sometimes heard banging, slaps and groans, as if someone in the next room was being beaten. Somehow, it didn't seem right.

Richard told my mom he had been fired from his job as an agent, but had gotten another job. We never saw him during the day, but as it turned out, that was because he was asleep in his room. When questioned about this, he said he had been sick. Mom went on with her life, but the disturbing sounds at night made her uneasy. Who was coming in the apartment? And what was going on?

Several times, when my mom got up in the middle of the night, she found the front door unlocked, even partially open. Then one day, early in the evening, Mom heard Richard yell from the hall, "Stay back! Stay back!" She ran and opened the door, and Richard ran in. Then, she quickly locked the door. Richard told her that some guy had followed him into the building and all the way up the stairs. He thought the guy had a knife.

Mom wanted Richard to call the police and report the guy, but Richard wouldn't do it, so Mom called someone in the building and told them there was a man inside who shouldn't be there. She was afraid for the other tenants. I didn't actually observe a lot of these events, but I heard about them later. And they all lead to something I did observe.

Now, after this, Mom asked Richard to PLEASE remember to lock the front door. She even made a big sign for the door, which said, "PLEASE LOCK THE DOOR!"

When we first moved into the room, my mom had observed a sort of bashed in portion of the old ceiling and asked about it.

"Oh, that's fine," everyone said. "It's been like that forever. No problem."

Then one night, Mom and I heard noises. Reaching over to me, Mom petted me, as she would often do in the night, and said, "Sabrina, I'm going to go see what's going on."

She went out to check the front door and found it unlocked and open. It was about one in the morning. This was after the man had followed Richard upstairs, and after Mom had specifically asked Richard to keep the apartment door locked. Mom closed the front door, locked it and came back to our room.

As she came through the entrance to our room, she was in such a rage she turned around and slammed the door shut with all her might. She was still standing with her face to the door and her hand on the knob, when a huge explosion sounded. It seemed as if the entire world was being blown apart. This was followed by an enormous plume of white smoke, which filled the entire room. All three of us cats ran for our lives. I don't know where Blossom and Theo went, but I got under the covers.

Apparently, when Mom slammed the door, she shook the dent in the ceiling just enough to move it. That sent a four-foot circle of hundred-year-old plaster with horsehair crashing to the floor.

Richard came running and all kinds of bedlam went on. Luckily, we were all fine. In a way, it was a blessing that the ceiling had come down. If it had fallen when one of us, or even my mom, was walking across the room, we most certainly would have been killed.

Now, the air was so thick with dust, we could barely breathe. Mom opened the window, and Richard brought a fan to try to pull the dusty air out of the room. Blossom and Theo were so terrified by this event; they remained hidden for a long while. Eventually, the management company came and fixed the ceiling.

Around this crazy time, Oliver told my mom he was going to Salt Lake City, Utah, to appear in Shakespeare's *Romeo and Juliet*. Oliver was the one person in that apartment Mom really trusted, and now she felt scared. When Oliver came home the day before he was to fly to Utah, he found my mom putting some kind of bolt on the inside of our door. She didn't want us locked in if she wasn't there, but she did want to be able to lock the door from the inside at night.

"You don't know how many nights I've been woken with my heart pounding in fear because of the noises in this apartment," she told Oliver.

"I think it's a good idea," he told my mom. "In fact, I'm thinking of putting a lock on my room."

Mom was out all day now, working, making money and paying her bills, but we had yet to see the worst of things.

One morning, when Mom got up to feed us, I didn't get up. I just couldn't. I felt so ill and weak; I could only raise my head. Mom tried to prod me, but I did not move. In a panic, she ran down the hall, looked in the yellow pages for a vet and picked up the phone. She dialed. Nothing happened. Then a message came on. The phone had been disconnected!

Mom was so worried about me; there was no time to deal with that problem. She put on her coat and ran down to the nearest pay phone about a block away, where she called a vet. They told her to come, so she ran back up the five flights of stairs, put me in a cage, and hurried back down with her heart pounding. I was just lying there in my cage.

"My poor little Sabrina," she said to me. "Hang in there, baby. It's okay. Mommy's taking you to the doctor."

One week prior to this, more than two feet of snow had fallen, followed only a few days later by another foot. The snow was piled high. This made it difficult to get from the sidewalk to the street and vice versa. Mom put us in a cab, and when we arrived at the corner nearest the West Side Veterinary Clinic, she had to place me on a four-foot high snowdrift and then climb over it on her hands and knees. Then, picking me up, she ran down the street to the hospital.

The vet looked at me and suggested a blood test. He was not really sure what was wrong, but he said I was very sick. I remember Mom and I sitting in the waiting room. I was in my cage, and she was on the chair next to me. It seemed so peaceful and safe.

Finally, the vet came out and told Mom the bad news. He said I had contracted a liver infection. My two liver rates, which if normal would have been no more than 75 and 60 respectively, were 1,044 and 1,055—an unheard-of level.

"I am really surprised she is even alive," the doctor told Mom. "If you had waited, she would not have made it. I am going to give her some antibiotics, but there is no guarantee she can survive this. We will just do the best we can."

The doctor also suggested additional tests, but already the bill was about $500, and Mom said she didn't know how much more she could afford. She had spent most of her savings coming to New York and taking classes. I know she felt terribly guilty because had she not brought me into the conditions under which we had been living, I would never have been so ill.

Mom brought me home, badly shaken. I felt horrible, but started on the antibiotics. It would be a long battle for me to feel well again.

Though I was too ill to care, Mom now confronted Richard; she was very angry at the situation. Then, she concentrated all her love on me. Since I was not eating, she went out to the butcher shop and got a big chicken and made the Jewish Chicken Soup I loved. At regular intervals, she fed me spoonfuls of chicken broth, which I swallowed gratefully. Sometimes she had to hold my poor, tired head in her hands as she carefully put the spoon to the side of my mouth and slowly poured the liquid down my throat.

Blossom and Theo were quiet and kind, letting me rest. They knew I was very ill. The doctor had said if I was to survive, I must be kept quiet with no stress. Any altercation that took place with Richard happened outside my hearing.

It did seem that Richard had lied to Mom, for she soon found that all the money she had given him—money for rent, electric, and phone bills—had not reached its destination. After that, Mom paid her bills directly, but this didn't really solve the problem. Shortly after this, there was a notice for each person living in the apartment, including Mom, demanding their presence in court for the non-payment of rent.

Since my mom was working during the day, and I was now so ill, she generally came into the room and went to bed about ten o'clock at night. During the night, there were many noises disturbing her, but she did not move. She only prayed for our safety. Now, she had the added worry of me and my health, but there would soon be another worry.

§

One Sunday morning, Mom decided to go into the living room to watch her favorite TV show, *The Eastenders*. As she approached the room, she saw a black curly head on the sofa, under the covers. She felt a little excited and wondered, "Is Oliver back already?"

Then, night after night, around 11 pm she heard the sound of chopping coming from the kitchen. What in the world was going on? In the daylight, she discovered that this chopping had been taking place in her new pots; they were scratched inside.

One night, she'd had enough of this and got up to see who was making this noise. There, in the kitchen, she discovered a foreign man who said he had been living there for several weeks. He was from Santo Domingo. Mom soon took her pots out of the kitchen and put them in our room.

When confronted, Richard told her that he'd let the guy stay there because his wife had died and he needed a place to live. Then, the guy started telling my mom he loved her, and several nights, we heard him pushing at the door, trying to get into our room. Despite my weakness, my eyes grew wide with fear. Mom lay next to me, her hand on my coat, silently praying that we would be safe.

At night, I ached so that I would moan and cry. I would ease my body up against my mom's, trying to gain comfort from her presence. She felt so sad for me. The doctor told her that what I had was like mononucleosis; so, of course, all my muscles and joints ached. To make me feel better, Mom would rub my back and my legs. I felt so appreciative of all her love and care.

It was while I lay so ill in this strange place that my mom and I became much closer and began to truly understand one another. It would be difficult to describe the beginnings of this. I can only say I knew I was totally dependent on her, and, at the same time, I knew she would do everything to care for me, just as a mother cat would.

It was during this illness that we started the counting game. In the past, whenever I sat next to Mom, I would sometimes tap her with my tail. Sometimes, when I was angry, I would slap her with it, showing my disapproval. She had often been annoyed with me for doing this, but now she came to realize that I was not trying to annoy her. Tapping her with my tail was really a way of expressing my feelings.

Following this realization, Mom and I began a new kind of communication—a language beyond words. It went like this: I would tap her twice with my tail, and she would respond in kind with her fingers. Then, she might tap me three or four times, and I would respond by tapping the exact number back to her. Later we would go up to six or more taps. In time, when I felt better, I would sometimes play with her and make her wait for my answer. Just when she thought I had not gotten it, I would give her the exact number she had given me back again.

In this manner of tail taps, we could also have a conversation. I would tell her, "Yes, everything is okay," or "No, I'm perturbed. I don't feel so well," or even "I love you." In time, our ability to exchange taps became one of our deepest forms of communication. We had been together nearly seven years, but our relationship went to a new level as we matched tap for tap.

My days were spent with Blossom and Theo. We were all basically stuck in that one room. We had a window, but there nothing outside it except a wall and other windows, so, in a manner, we hibernated in this room. Outside our door were those two dogs, which none of us really wanted to see. In this strange situation, at least we had each other. That was some comfort.

As things began to occur in the apartment, Mom was in communication with Oliver in Utah. She let him know what was going on, because he was in danger of losing his place to live as well. From my mom's description of something she found in the bathroom, Oliver explained what was really going on—drugs. I didn't know what it was, but I knew it was serious and my mom knew we had to get out of there. Oliver said he'd be back in a couple of weeks. He hoped my mom would wait for his return.

Meanwhile, Richard said he was going to be honest. "Yeah," my mom said, "honest about sleeping all-day and waiting by the window at night; watching Columbus Avenue for the drug dealer to arrive."

Even sadder than our situation was the fact Richard no longer cared about his two little dogs. He rarely took them out for a walk, and when they peed on the floor as a result, he beat them. I could hear them crying through the door. My mom started walking the dogs. She pitied them and she wasn't sure what else she should do. I thought they were really nice little dogs.

Mom told us she was going to find us a better place to live. It took a little while, but at the end of February, Mom packed us up and said we were moving to another apartment. She was so happy to be leaving. She hired a small truck and a driver to take us to the new apartment.

We were taking the bed with us. Mom figured we'd lost our deposit, and it was the least we should get. Richard begged her to pay him, even ten dollars for it, but she refused. She knew the money was only going to go for drugs. Then, while Mom went downstairs with some of her packages, I saw Richard come in our room, go into the closet, and take her beloved Pentax camera. Of course, I couldn't tell her. She had to find that out herself. But by then, it was too late.

The new place was about 100 blocks away, at the top of Manhattan. An actress, just off tour, needed a temporary roommate. She also had a big black dog living there. Theo didn't like that dog. He thought he had to protect us girls, and whenever he got the chance, he would charge into the next room and try to attack the dog. I think the dog was okay.

Our room had two doors. One went into the kitchen; the other went to the living room. It was a nice sized room with a whole corner of windows that looked out on a garden. In the daytime, you could hear singing and instruments being played. We were happy to be there. And it was very clean.

Mom continued to care for me. I had gone through several courses of antibiotics, and the vet told her that he was really surprised I was still alive. However, I kept having relapses with fever and feeling not so good. Mom got to the point she could see it coming. Someone told her that garlic and vitamin E were good. So, instead of going back to the doctor for another prescription of antibiotics, which was expensive and messing my stomach up, Mom began to make pills of slightly boiled garlic put inside vitamin E capsules. I would get one a day for a few days in a row, and that seemed to do the trick.

Warning: Although this remedy appears to have helped Sabrina, in recent years it has been discovered that garlic can be dangerous for cats. It may cause blood clots or leukemia. More research is needed. ***Use at your own peril.***

In addition, Mom continued to feed me Jewish Chicken Soup. Most of the time, I was able to eat on my own, but sometimes I still needed help. I also began to take barley greens. They came in the form of a green powder that Mom mixed with water. She'd feed this chlorophyll drink to me by the spoonful. I'd get about three or four or five spoons in the morning and a few at night. At first I hated it. It tasted like liquid grass. Eventually, I got used to it. Every time Mom brought the spoon up to my mouth she'd say, "Come on now, Sabrina. Take this so you can be a healthy girl."

I listened to her and took it. Apparently, her mother, Marian, had heard that barley greens cleanse the blood. This may have been an important factor in my recovery.

During this difficult time, my mother showed me such love and compassion. I loved her so much for that, and I knew she loved me just as much. We had been through hell together, and now, we were hoping for music and happiness.

Each night after work, Mom came home and practiced the songs for her show. Blossom, Theo and I were her audience. She would try things out on us, to see if we liked them, and I'd let her know whether I thought it was good or not. Too loud or harsh, and I'd frown. Nice and sweet, with good tone and pitch, and I'd close my eyes, smiling with pleasure.

Theo was something else though. He seemed to think Mom's singing was some kind of cat song just for him. She'd have to push him off just so she could rehearse.

Life was beautiful and serene in our room at the top of Manhattan. We watched the cherry blossoms bloom on the trees outside our windows. There was a window seat over the heater where Blossom liked to sit and watch the life below. The blossoms of April led quickly to May. Finally, when it was time for our mother to do her show, she got sick, but she did it anyway.

The day after it was over, her friends, who had come up from Washington, D.C. to see the show, loaded our things in their van and drove us back home. We cats weren't quite sure where we were going as they drove through New Jersey, Delaware and Maryland, but the car was filled with happy conversation. So, after a while we calmed down.

I cannot tell you how happy I was as my mother carried me up the steps and through the door of our home on "G" Street. There was the same furniture, the same warm yellow-papered walls and brown carpet. I was home at last! And on the weekends, I was allowed once again to go out on the brick patio and climb up the old wooden fence to the brick wall. There I could sit as I used to, listening to the birds sing and watching life in the gardens below. This was my true home—all I had known and all I ever wanted to know.

Picture of our home on "G" Street SE

Chapter 11

Return to D.C.

Back in Washington, D.C. life seemed normal. Michelle went to work in an office and came home each day at the same time. We cats, exhausted by all we had experienced, spent most of our time calmly resting in the upstairs bedroom.

There was one thing, however, that was not so normal. Familiar things began to disappear out of the house. Now, during our years in the house on Capitol Hill, many items had been added to our home, and some of these items were things we didn't really need. Still, when our dining room table and chairs disappeared, it seemed very odd indeed. It turned out that as a result of our New York adventure, Mom owed a great deal of money, and she was selling these things to pay her debts. Sometimes on the weekend, she would even put things out in front of the house and try to sell them.

One day, when Mom was having one of her yard sales, a short woman with dark hair stopped to talk with her. The woman said she was from California and had come to Washington, D.C. to learn how to become a Congresswoman. She was looking for a place to live. A short time after this, we had a vacancy in our house, and Mom called the woman, who quickly accepted her offer to rent the middle room.

The woman, whom I will call "Vera," seemed to be very nice, neat and quiet. She was born in Mexico, but had raised her children in California. Mom left our old bed and one of our bookshelves in the bedroom for Vera, as she had no furniture.

Now, one of the things I haven't told you about is a kind of scourge we suffered in summertime. Washington, D.C. is sort of a tropical place, and every year from late spring to early autumn, we had what they call, "no see-ums." These are bugs that bit you like fleas, but you never see them. They seem to be invisible. They come out late in the day. When we lived in D.C., even if you stood for only a moment on the front steps by the garden or walked along the path, they would jump on you and bite your legs.

As for us cats, well, they got on us, and when we came inside the house, they quickly spread to the carpet. Since no one could see them, they were really difficult to fight! We were constantly jumping up and biting ourselves, trying to get rid of these bugs. Even Mom was not exempt. After the "no see-ums" bit her, she had big, red bumps all over her feet and legs. By the middle of the summer, she was scratching so much her legs were swollen and bleeding.

After a couple of years suffering like this, Mom found a remedy to stop the invasion. First, in late May or early June, she'd steam clean the carpets. She did this again in September. Then, during the summer, she made us cats take baths.

To start out, Mom would put all of us in a room. Then, one by one, she'd take us into the bathroom and wash us. I was usually the first one. She'd bring me in while she had the water running in the tub, and I would think, "Oh, no! I'm going to take a bath!" I really didn't want to take a bath, but remember water didn't bother me too much, so I went along with it.

Once I was soaking wet, Mom took some liquid sudsy stuff for cats and started rubbing it all over my body. This part actually felt pretty good, especially when it was really hot outside; the water cooled me down. Once I was all soapy, I was allowed to get out of the tub and sit on the floor or in the window, while I waited, as Mom said, for the soap to "kill the no see-ums."

Then came the part I hated most of all. Mom would start the water running again as she put me back in the tub. After most of the soap was off, she would make me get under the running water. It may have seemed like only a little water to her, but to me it was a huge waterfall! I guess she had a good reason for doing this, but there never seemed to be a good enough reason to me. It was scary, and I often felt as if I was going to be drowned. In time, Mom realized that using a little bucket to pour water over my back and the back of my head (while she held my ears shut) was a whole lot easier and less frightening.

Once the soap was gone, Mom squeezed me to get all the water out of my fur. Then, she'd wrap me in a towel, and rub me all over. Finally, after all this, she would send me out of the bathroom to dry on my own.

Blossom was usually next. When it came to taking baths, she was the worst. Even before she got wet, she started screaming and howling as if she were being murdered. The bathroom window was on the side of the house facing our neighbor's home. Echoing down this narrow alley, Blossom's voice was heard throughout the neighborhood. Later, Mom would have to explain to the neighbors she was not torturing her cat.

After we were all finished with our baths, Mom would come out of the bathroom soaking wet. By this time, we were all sitting in the sun, licking ourselves dry. Mom combed our fur and rubbed the parts of us that were still wet. On very hot days, it didn't take us long to dry.

While I was probably the only cat that didn't protest taking a bath, by the time Mom wanted to comb me, I had had enough. I would tell her, "I can do this myself! Leave me alone!" If the message wasn't clear, I'd give her a bite or a scratch. In those days, she really could test my patience.

Anyway, the year Vera moved in was a particularly bad year for "no see-ums." For one reason or another, Mom had not been able to get rid of them as well as she wanted, but she had learned to protect herself from most of the bug bites by coating her legs with olive oil soap. Vera, however, had been in the house only one night when she told Mom she was getting bit.

Mom told Vera she would take care of it. I think she tried, but Vera was still getting bit. One or two days after speaking to Mom, Vera dipped a mop in full strength bleach and started dragging it through the house. The windows must have been closed that day because in a short time the house was filled with the bleach fumes. This was the situation when Mom came home from work. She almost had an asthma attack and had to run outside. I started to get sick too; in fact, all of us cats were sneezing and coughing.

After Mom had opened the windows, Vera told her, "Oh, bleach is really good for your lungs. It opens them up." Then she said, "I'm going to put bleach on the carpet every week so there will be no more bugs and it will be sterilized from those cats." Imagine that! She blamed us for the "no see-um," and thought we were dirty!

Mom told Vera she wasn't going to put bleach on the carpet anymore—that it was NOT healthy! Besides, she didn't want us cats getting bleach on our feet! After that, she took all three of us into the bathroom, put our paws under running water, and then dried them. She was afraid we might lick the bleach off our paws.

I don't know what happened after that, but I guess Mom got rid of the bugs. I think Vera also got some poison and sprayed her room with it. I recall a hissing sound and a very odd odor coming from under her door. With all the strange goings on in the house, Mom decided it might be better if we stayed locked in our room while she was at work.

A short time after this, I was sitting in our bedroom window, when I noticed Vera walking down the street. There was a bunch of stuff piled in front of the big, brick apartment house across the street, and I saw Vera walk over, look at it and, then, begin dragging things one by one across the street and up the steps to our house.

When Mom came home that night, she saw some stuff lying in our front yard. Some of it was even lying on top of the flowers she had planted in our garden. She was mad about that. I heard her grumbling as she removed the things. Then, she came up the steps into the dark house. There was not a light on in the place, though I knew Vera was home.

When Mom let us out for dinner, Blossom, Theo and I rushed downstairs, eager to see what was going on. Turning into the living room, and then into the dining room, we were very surprised to find both rooms completely filled with the strange stuff I had seen Vera dragging across the street. We took our time checking it out. Some of it had a very, peculiar odor.

As soon as Mom had given us our dinner, she went up and knocked on Vera's door and asked her what was going on. Vera said she'd found these

Mom sitting on the steps of our "G" Street home

things. "Don't you want them?" she asked. "No," said Mom, "I want you to take them out of the house."

Shortly after dinner, I was sitting on the small table in the living room cleaning myself, when there was a knock on the door. Mom answered it, and there was a very nice looking black man on the landing. He greeted her politely and, after introducing himself, said, "I live across the street, and due to a mix up with the landlord—he said I hadn't paid my rent, but I have—I came home from work to find the locks on my apartment changed and some of my things on the street. One of my neighbors told me that she saw some lady from across the street take my belongings. I see some of them in your front garden."

"Oh, I'm so sorry," said Mom, "the woman who rents a room in my house did that. Your things are here, and you are very welcome to take them back."

"Well, I really appreciate that," said the man, "Legally, once they evict you in D.C. you have three days to get your belongings. No one is supposed to touch them during that time. I have a brand new TV and other things I haven't even finished paying for."

"Oh, no!" said Mom, "I don't want them. I got home and was wondering where they came from. This woman just moved here from California. I guess she didn't know."

"I'm sorry I won't be able to take them today. This is a terrible mess. I will have to get a truck and someone to help me move them. Can I come back tomorrow?"

"That's fine."

I could tell as Mom shut the door, that she was greatly relieved the man would soon be taking his things out of our house. The house had been nice, clean and neat. Now it was a mess. You could barely walk from one room to the next.

Only a moment after Mom closed the door, Vera appeared around the corner. She seemed very anxious and told Mom, "I was going to donate these things to the homeless shelter for the poor."

"But these things belong to that man, and he is homeless!" said Mom.

"I found them, and now they are mine," Vera insisted. With that, she walked out of the room in a huff.

"These things belong to someone else," Mom called after her. "This is my house, and I don't want them here!"

I could tell Mom was getting exasperated. I think she knew she had made a mistake renting to Vera. If she didn't know then, she soon would.

The next evening, I was sitting on my favorite perch in the front window. Just as the sun was about to set, I saw the man who owned the things Vera had taken come up our front steps and knock on the door. Mom was glad to see him. Vera was out of the house at that moment, and this would make things a lot easier. The man came in and started loading up his TV, chairs, lamps and everything else. You have no idea how much of his stuff was in our house!

Only a few minutes after the man began loading his things in the truck outside, I looked down the block, and there was Vera, walking toward our house. It seemed like she walked a little bit faster when she saw the stuff going out of the house. She arrived at the gate just as the man was walking out the door with one of his lamps. I could hear her talking.

"I'm going to call the police. You are trespassing."

My mom heard her too and went to the door to meet her as she came up the steps.

"This is my property, and he is not trespassing!"

Vera stomped by Mom and went upstairs to her room. Oh my! What was going to happen next?

Well, nothing happened that day. The man got the rest of his things while Vera stayed in her room, and that was that.

$$\mathfrak{s}$$

For a while, things were quiet in our house. Vera went out for part of the day, and when she returned, she went to her room and shut the door. Now, the front parlor was always dark. We no longer lingered there as before. We went to the kitchen to eat and then hung out in the upstairs bedroom with our mom. I was always eager to go upstairs and stay behind closed doors. I just didn't feel like being bothered by cats or people.

$$\mathfrak{s}$$

A few weeks after the events I just described, Steve, our political roommate, came to Mom and told her that soon he would be out on the campaign trail. He thought he would be gone for at least two months. His boss was running for governor, and he was going to be very busy. Meanwhile, Vera had not paid the last month's rent or any of her bills. Mom began to worry about living alone with a crazy lady, who was not paying her share of the expenses.

The first time Mom asked Vera when she was going to pay the money she owed, she said, "I don't know. I will have to ask the priest whether I should pay you or not."

I guess Vera was mad about the things Mom allowed the man to take back, but I really don't know. The next time Mom spoke to Vera was on the Sunday before Steve left. This time, when she asked about the bills, Vera pointed to her mouth and acted like she was gargling. Then, she walked down the stairs and out the door.

Vera started coming in late at night to avoid everyone. So, Mom put a written warning under her door, stating that she must pay her rent in one week, or move. In the meantime, Vera had collected more stuff off the street and brought it into our house. Some of it was very dirty.

Finally, after doing some research, Mom knew what she had to do. One Sunday morning, she told Blossom and Theo they had to stay in the bedroom. I was the only one allowed downstairs. She seemed concerned about my presence, but I think she wanted me there for moral support. For several days, I had noticed she was very nervous. This Sunday, as she sat at the kitchen table and dialed a number on the phone, her hands were shaking.

A few minutes later, there was a knock on the front door. Mom went to open it, and two policemen came in. They walked with heavy feet up our stairs and knocked on Vera's door. Then I heard them say, "M'am, it's the police. You have been asked to leave the premises, and we are here to escort you out."

Vera didn't answer right away. When she did, she didn't want to open the door. I guess she told them she lived there and had a right to be there, but they told her she didn't have a lease or any legal right to stay. She was basically a guest who had been asked to leave. The policemen gave Vera five minutes to pack up some things. They told her at the end of that time, they would accompany her outside. She would be able to return another day to get the rest of her things, but she would need a police escort and she would have to take everything at once.

While all this was going on, Mom stayed hidden in the kitchen, pacing nervously back and forth. We heard the police raise their voices to Vera, telling her that she had to get ready to leave with the door open. They had to see what she was doing. For a few minutes, it was kind of intense and scary.

Then, one of the policemen came downstairs and gave Mom Vera's key to the front door. He told Mom he thought Vera was a little crazy and assured her that she was doing the right thing by getting Vera out. He said, "I have seen cases like her before."

Vera did not want to leave and protested all the way. Finally, the two policemen escorted her out the front door and down the steps to the sidewalk. Still shaking, Mom locked the front door. Later, I heard her tell a friend that putting Vera out was one of the hardest things she had ever done. Still, we all felt greatly relieved with her out of the house. Now, we could relax, and, once again, our house seemed a pleasant and peaceful place.

Things with Vera weren't completely finished, however. On many occasions after that, from my window seat, I would see her walking slowly down the street, gazing up out our house. Several times, she called and left threatening messages on our answering machine, but it was just talk.

After many weeks, Vera finally returned with a police escort and took the rest of her things out of the room. One day, while waiting for Vera to return, Mom looked in the room, and it was a mess. It held a lot of things that obviously did not belong to her. When Vera returned, she wanted to linger in the house, but the policemen told her she had to finish and get out. They had more important things to do.

After that, Mom said she was only going to rent to people who worked on Capitol Hill, and had professional references.

During this time, our life was not always laden with tension and unhappiness. Mom continued to sing and listen to interesting music. It was during this time that she began to play some country music recordings for us by a mother and daughter team called "The Judds." We enjoyed them a lot. She also went to many shows with her good friend, Randy, and began working on some new music projects. These things kept her busy and happy, which of course kept us cats happy as well.

While we lived on "G" Street, Mom had many affectionate names for us cats, me in particular. She said it was because we lived in the South that she came up with these names. I think she picked up some of them from her friends. One name she used just to be sweet with me (don't laugh) was "Baby-cakes." Later, she sometimes called me "Breenie-cakes." I liked it when Mom called me these names because I knew it meant love. It was just a personal thing between me and my mom.

As for my health, I continued to have some traces of liver disease, and Mom continued to worry about it. In November of that year, she took me to a holistic veterinarian in Maryland, who took my blood and an x-ray of my liver. Mom brought me home from that visit with all kinds of vitamins and powders. They must have helped me because I don't remember having any more bouts of liver illness after that.

Because of all the attention on my health and an illness that had nothing to do with age, no one really thought about how old I was. Mom said that cats are considered seniors by the time they are seven, but I was now seven and feeling in my prime. It seemed the only thing that aged me were the many traumatic experiences I had been through. And because of those experiences, all I really wanted was peace and quiet.

After the elections in November, Steve told us he was moving back to Pennsylvania. He had never been that close to us, but he was a nice, quiet guy, so we were all sorry to see him go. After Steve left, we had a couple of female roommates move in. Mom really didn't get along with them that well, so we moved back into the middle room for a while, and just lived our quiet lives.

In June of 1995, I went back to visit my original vet at Jane's Veterinary on 8th Street. To get there, Mom put me in my cage and loaded it on her luggage cart. Then, away we went! It was a bumpy ride, but interesting to be able to see at all the old houses along the way. Once again, I had to take a blood test, about which I was not thrilled. The only thing I didn't know was why.

Two days later, I went back to Jane's Veterinary Clinic. They took me in the back room and put a mask on my face. After that, I don't remember

Contentment

anything, but when I woke up, my mouth felt different. It was fresh and silky smooth. Mom said I had had my teeth cleaned.

Shortly after this experience, my mom took a trip to Grand Rapids, Minnesota, where she sang at *The Judy Garland Festival.* When she returned, she told us we were going back to New York. She promised that this trip would be much better than the last. Nevertheless, I was not pleased. When she came to put me in my cage, I hissed at her and told her off. I did not want to go, but Mom was insistent. She was going, and she was not going to leave me behind. Blossom and Theo seemed more docile about the whole thing, but I always did know my mind.

Chapter 12
Music and My Favorite Singer

This time when we went to New York, Mom got a car and drove it herself. She put a lot of stuff in that car. By the time it was packed and we had ridden a few hours, Mom was tired. She took us to a motel in Delaware, and we slept there for one night. We arrived in New York City on a hot, sunny, noisy day. There were horns honking and people yelling.

The apartment we stayed in belonged to a friend of a friend. It was a spacious two-room affair with big windows in each room and a lot of light. The bedroom was on the street side of the apartment, and there was constant noise from the city, so I spent most of my time in the back room. Although it was not home, the place was comfortable, clean and safe. Mom brought some covers from D.C. to put on the furniture so it would feel like home. Despite all the things I didn't like, I had to smile because my mother was so happy and practiced her singing for us all the time.

It was during this period that my mother brought home the recordings of a singer I would grow to love. Her name was Nancy LaMott. There was something about Nancy's voice that called to me. She sang with a deep, throaty tone. But then, suddenly and just as easily, her voice became light and delicate, like a bird. Most importantly, Nancy sang from the heart.

Every time my mom played Nancy LaMott's recordings, I felt happy. Mom had two recordings by Nancy, and for a while, she played them every night before we went to sleep. Those recordings were the highlight of my day.

As a small aside, Mom actually met Nancy during this time, though she never told her how much I liked her. My love for her singing would grow

*A photo of my favorite
singer, Nancy LaMott,
by Stephen Mosher*

over the years. Sadly, none of us knew how sick Nancy was. She passed away that year, in December of 1995. No one could believe that someone so young and alive, who sang with such passion, could so suddenly be gone. Even though Nancy is gone from this world, her recordings have continued to be a joy in my life.

Meanwhile, my mom's life revolved more and more around music and performing. She was always either practicing or dressing up and going out to sing. While she didn't spend as much time with us as before, there was an air of excitement and happiness in our apartment that had been lacking during our last year in Washington, D.C. It was as if Mom had become young again.

Like all cats (and people who are wise), I lived in the moment. Now that I was getting older, I found there was more to enjoy in life than running around the neighborhood. Mom, Blossom, Theo and I were a family who stayed together and had good music. Who could ask for more?

Chapter 13

Living in New York,
Home Is Where the Heart Is

After three months in the apartment on West 55th Street, it was time for us to move out. My mom was determined to stay in New York City, and after much searching, she found a one-room sublet down on West 23rd Street. In the past, even when we stayed indoors most of the time, Blossom, Theo and I always had a lot of room to roam. Now, as you can imagine, moving into a tightly packed studio apartment was tough.

The one saving grace of this apartment was the fact that we had an out-door playground. It seems the front of the building we were living in was five or six stories high, but the back of the first floor was only one story. We lived on the second floor, so our windows opened onto the first floor roof, which had a wall around the edge, so you couldn't fall off. In good weather, Mom let us go out the window to run around. Sometimes, we just sat out there in the sun. Mom and the other neighbors did this as well. The roof was the one thing that kept us cats from being totally crazy.

Besides our roof, the neighboring building had a penthouse, which I was quick to discover. There was a garden and all sorts of nice furniture up there. With little trouble I could jump the wall and go over to the pent-house. I told you I always liked the finest things, and this penthouse was quite something, especially for a place in the city. I even found some grass to eat. With these advantages, my opinion of life in New York changed; it didn't seem so bad after all.

Waiting for Mom to come home to our N.Y. apartment

Soon after we moved into our new apartment, my mom decided to give up our Washington, D.C. home once and for all. She wanted to stay in New York and see what would happen with her singing. So, on many weekends, she had someone to feed us while she went down to our old house and did some packing.

Then came the day when she went down for one last time, to clean the house and say goodbye. How I wished I could go too, but she knew it would break my heart to see our house again and have to leave. What Mom didn't know was that it would break her heart as well. She told me later that she cried hard during those final days of saying goodbye to our home, the home which had been such a happy place for so many years. But it was then that she learned, just as I did, that home is where the heart is. Together, Mom, Blossom, Theo and I were a family, so in the end, it didn't matter where we went—as long as we were together.

Some months after the house in Washington, D.C. had been packed up, our mother hired a truck and moved our things out of storage into our one-room apartment. As you can imagine, it was pretty crowded in there. Boxes lined the walls from floor to ceiling, with the bookcases being used to divide the studio into two-rooms. Although our place was crowded, it had a homey air for us. In addition, Mom hoped that the separation of the room would give me a little more privacy. She was aware that Theo and I did not get along, but she really didn't know how bad the situation had become.

I had always disliked Theo on principle. He was a big, restless cat, who felt he had to be the lord of our domain. Just the appearance of his fat face with the big green eyes filled me with hatred and dread. I would hiss, growl and run whenever I saw him. Likely, our close quarters intensified the difficulties between us. In recent months, Theo had taken steps to become

Theo, my cat nemesis

proactive toward me. Now, when I hissed, he ran at me and tried to attack me. One time, he actually rolled me across the floor like a ball, while my mother screamed.

Mom tried not to take sides. She yelled at Theo, but she was also critical of me. She told me not to run, but that was easy for her to say. Theo was twice my size and five years younger. As time went on, the mere sight of him filled me with terror. When Mom was not around, it became high priority for me to remain hidden. I would run as quickly as I could to a safe place in a space where Theo could not reach me. I often crammed myself between the wall and the wooden futon bed-frame, or behind some boxes, and I'd lie there cramped up all day, if need be, until Mom came home.

There was another thing my mother didn't know, although I think she found it out later. Our apartment sat over a dry cleaning store, and during the day, when Mom was at work, the fumes from the store would come up through the floor into our apartment. This meant that as I lay hidden in my cramped space, I was stuck there, breathing the fumes. They were rather intoxicating, but at the time certainly preferable to dealing with Theo. Although it wasn't evident right away, these dry cleaning fumes may have been one of the causes of the ill health I have suffered from so intensely in my later years.

During this time, my mother became quite ill as well. She had collapsed the day we moved into this apartment. It had been terribly hot that day, and she had taken trip after trip, moving all our things by herself, from one apartment to the other. I heard that something was not right with her heart after this, so she stayed home with us for quite a while, taking long naps in the day and sleeping ten or more hours at night. Of course, during the time she was home, peace reigned among us cats. Even so, I often felt compelled to hide.

That December, Mom decided she wanted to be with her mother and the rest of her family for Christmas. Our apartment cost a lot of money; so, she sublet it to a man from Iceland for about a month. In return for less rent, the man agreed to take care of Theo and Blossom.

As for me, because Mom was always concerned about my health, as well as the situation with Theo, she decided I should travel with her to California. This time, I traveled in a small, flat cage that went inside the plane, under the seat in front of her. During this trip, she never let me out of her sight. Despite the cramped quarters, being able to be inside the plane meant that my trip was much nicer and much easier.

California was nice and warm, and no one bothered me in the front room with the big window. Once in a while, I'd see my granddaughter, Polly, but I let her know I didn't want to be bothered. She agreed and went on her way, swooshing that big, plumey, white tail of hers.

Shortly before we arrived in California, there had been a snowstorm in New York that shut down all the airports. On our return in January, as the cab drove us back to 23rd Street, the snow was coming down in big, thick flakes. It snowed all night and all the next day. By the following day, the snow was halfway up our window, and the entire city was shut down. Mom kept saying, "Thank God we got home, Sabrina! Thank God we're not stuck in an airport!"

Well, as a cat, I was not doing all the running around my mom was doing. I didn't go out to sing or to work or to meet a man and fall in love. There was just the momentary time on the neighbor's penthouse roof. A lot of my time also was spent looking out the window at the apartment buildings across the way, with ivy growing on the walls, and the church steeple beyond. Being a cat, I had no thought of the past or the future—only the singular stirring that there might be a better life beyond. And there was.

Chapter 14
Life in Jersey City

O n Thanksgiving Day 1996, we moved lock, stock and barrel—as they say—to a big apartment in Jersey City, New Jersey. Early in the morning that day some men came and took everything out of our 23rd Street apartment. Mom went with them, leaving us cats somewhat traumatized. Many hours later, she returned. We were put in our cages, which were placed one on top of the other and strapped to her luggage carrier. Then, away we went rolling down the sidewalks of New York City. After traveling a short distance, we descended into an underground tunnel. This place is known in New York as "the subway."

While we were in the tunnel, a huge wind began to blow followed by a distant rumble. Suddenly, a monster came roaring out of the dark. The monster had doors on its side, which opened, and to our surprise, Mom took us inside. This was our first trip on a train, and it was quite an experience! Unlike a plane, the inside was very well lit, but it was a rough ride. We bounced up and down, as the room rattled, squeaked and roared. Every once in a while, there would be a dinging sound, and the doors would open. Some people got off, and others got on. Then, the doors closed, and the train started up again. After this happened a few times, the doors opened once again and Mom rolled us out of the train and up some moving steps to a wide-open area. We were now in Jersey City.

After traveling only a block from the train station, we arrived in front of a small garden with a tall house. Mom opened the gate and took us up the path to the front door, which she unlocked. On entering the door, we found ourselves in a little hallway with two more doors. One door stood at the top of several steps, and this was the one we entered. Mom carried us partway up a narrow staircase, then put our cages down on the landing, and opened the doors, encouraging us to come out. She wanted us to walk the rest of the way up by ourselves.

Blossom, Theo and I spent a few minutes sniffing around, and then scampered up the steps after our mother. The stairs turned a corner and went up a few more steps, stopping in front of a door. This door opened and led to another narrow hallway.

On one side of the hall, was an empty room with a long window. At the other end was a kitchen. Another door led to a bathroom, and directly opposite that door was the entrance to the large square room, which would be our living room. With the exception of the cool brick ceramic tiled floors of the kitchen and bathroom, all the other rooms were covered with soft white carpeting.

Exploring our new home, I found that everywhere I went there were piles and piles of boxes. I soon discovered that all these boxes—and the furniture hiding behind them—contained our old, familiar belongings from "G" Street and New York City. There were boxes with books, dishes, pictures and more. Blossom, Theo, and I spent days exploring these things. Since we were all thrown off-balance with the fascination of this new place, there would be no fighting between Theo and me for a while. It would take months for Mom to unpack everything, and find places to put it.

In New Jersey, Blossom and Theo lived their life, and I lived mine.

Our new apartment took the entire top floor of the old house in Jersey City. The living room was a nice sized space with two windows looking out at a huge tree, a garden, and many other yards beyond. The view from here was most fascinating to me. There were squirrels, cats, dogs, and even possums out those windows. I would often look out to see a cat climbing over the back fence, as a big lady in the next yard called, "Baa-by! Here, Baby! Here, kitty-kitty-kitty!"

In the morning, there was beautiful sunshine in this room. My mom placed the old sideboard under the window, and this was where I chose to eat most of my meals. In this spot I could sit and enjoy the life below as I munched on chicken and biscuits. I needed to feel secure while I ate, so from this point on, I always dined on high places like tables or cabinets. Blossom and Theo continued to eat their meals on the kitchen floor.

Our new apartment had one unique feature—a window opening between the kitchen and living room. The television was placed on the counter in this window space, and when I wanted to, I could walk through to check on what was cooking in the kitchen.

There was one more room in this apartment and that was our bedroom. Opposite the living room windows were a set of double doors. Inside these doors (and on either side of them) were two large closets. Beyond that narrow entrance was a huge room with a sealed fireplace, long mantel, and a bay consisting of five windows. Mom put some boxes under these windows and this gave us cats a place to sit and look out. There were trees in front of the windows and a lot of birds in those trees. Blossom used to sit there all the time and talk to the birds in the funny way we cats speak to our prey.

The windows, however, had two drawbacks. In the daytime, the little street outside had plenty of traffic and was very noisy with people yelling. Furthermore, in winter, the cold air came through the cracks, making it a very uncomfortable place to be. All in all, I much preferred the living room windows at the back of the house.

After being so cramped up in our New York apartment, we all felt quite happy in this spacious New Jersey apartment. For the first month, only Mom and we cats lived there. Then, in the second month, we were joined by a young student from China. Zhe Chang moved into the small bedroom by the front door. Zhe (pronounced Tszee) was a very sweet guy. I remember he made a little party for my mom one night and served shrimp. He also agreed to take care of us when Mom had to go out of town.

One of the reasons Mom chose this apartment, besides the fact that you could get more for your money with two-bedrooms than one, was because she wanted to be sure there would always be someone at home to care for us if she needed to go out of town. That was one of the deals with the room-mates—they had to be willing to feed us.

Zhe did not stay with us too long. His father was ill, and after about six months, he returned home to China. After Zhe, a new Chinese room-mate moved in and took his place. This fellow had graduated from school in Texas, and he had an odd accent. Mom called it a "Texas-Chinese accent." Charlie, as we called him, not only had a strange accent, but he was rather an odd fellow.

Charlie was working in the stock market and believed he was going to be rich very soon. At night, he would come into the living room and pace back and forth while my mom tried to watch TV. He would do this until she said she was finished with her show and he could watch whatever he wanted. Then, he would sit and eat his food, sucking it and making all kinds of noise. Mom found she could not eat with him.

I never had to be cared for by Charlie, but I know Blossom and Theo did. Blossom said she had a tough time with him because she insisted on a clean toilet box, and Charlie never would clean it. In fact, he didn't care if she ended up using the bathmat or floor to pee on. He just didn't seem to care about anything.

Unlike our house in Washington, D.C., the roommates in this apart-ment mostly lived their own lives, but I am getting ahead of myself here. Besides, I have much more important things to tell you about the years we lived in Jersey City.

Once the living room in our new apartment was set up, it appeared that our mother was getting ready to do a show. She was writing constantly now and practicing songs. She also had a little girl named Carissa come in to rehearse. Carissa was a cute little girl with a beautiful voice, and she learned very fast.

We cats enjoyed these musical rehearsals and the company. In fact, during this time, our company was so nice even Blossom began to come around. She was still shy, but not as afraid as she had been. She especially seemed to enjoy the children. In fact, as the years went by in Jersey City, Blossom became fairly comfortable with strangers. She even let Mom approach her and pick her up.

As for Theo—I know you will think I'm prejudiced, but he was always a hog for attention. In Washington, whenever we had company he used to try to slide down the banister. Then, he would get up on one of the little banister balls and with all four feet positioned tightly together, turn around in a circle. All this for attention!

During our years in Jersey City, when anyone came to visit, Theo always acted as if they had come to see him. He would jump in their laps and insist that they focus on him, somewhat like a dog. I have to say, he was very annoying to me in this way. I understood the company was there to see Mom or our roommates. I was always happy to greet anyone who spoke to me, but if the visitors were busy, I would sit there quietly and politely, happy to be a pleasant presence. After many years of Theo's behavior, I eventually grew tired of it and excused myself from most of the welcoming duties in our house.

In the New Jersey apartment, as before, I slept on my pillow, which was located between the wall and my mom's head. This way, I always felt safe and never had to worry about Theo approaching me in the night. I know he wanted to sleep up on the pillows too. He was always very upset when Mom sent him back to the bottom of the bed with Blossom. He was really jealous of me and grumbled about the fact that he couldn't sleep there, but Mom knew my place was with her. There was no question about that.

Nighttime was the time when my mom and I had the most communication. Sometimes, she'd play the "tail-tap" game and pet me. I always knew if she was happy or sad or worried, and I always tried to assure her that things were going to be okay. I know she felt comforted by my love. I would purr my happiness during these late nights. I was so pleased and content to be with her, and so grateful she had helped me feel well again.

As the months went by in Jersey City, Mom seemed busier than ever. She was always working, rehearsing, writing, and practicing her singing, as well as going out to meet people and perform around New York City. At home, I often sat by her side, or just above her on the futon, while she talked on the phone, watched TV, or sang. When I had had enough, I'd go into the other room and sit by myself. By now, the remnants of my liver disease had vanished and with our pleasant new apartment, I was feeling pretty good.

In April of 1997, Mom went to California to visit her mother. I know she thought I would be alright while she was gone—at that time, Zhe was there to care for us—but little did she know the wars Theo and I were still having. One day, as I ran across the bed to escape him, he jumped me and knocked me against the wall, splitting the tip of my ear in two. After that, except for when Zhe fed us, I stayed in the space between the wall and the bed, hoping and praying that Theo would forget about me and leave me alone.

When Mom returned from California and discovered my blood on the bedroom wall, she was very upset. She could see how badly my ear had been split and how stressed I was. But while she was angry with Theo, she told me I had to take some of the blame. I didn't like it, but I listened to her explanation of how my behavior aggravated him. She knew something had to change.

"Theo has been punished enough for his bad behavior," my mom told me. "Your hisses and running away from him only incite him to attack you. Sabrina, if you stand up to him, he will back down and leave you alone because, basically, Theo is a good cat."

I didn't agree with that and, while I listened, I was not yet ready to test her theory. Instead, I continued to do what I knew how to do, and that was to run, screaming as loudly as I could.

To keep the fighting (and my aggravation) down, when Mom was not home to supervise us, she put Theo and Blossom in one room, and me in the other. She also bought a bolt and put it on the French doors between the living room and bedroom, so that Blossom, who was a master door opener, could not open the doors—Blossom knew how to turn doorknobs and fiddle with locks. So now, finally, when Mom was not at home, I was able to relax and enjoy myself. This cut back greatly on my stress.

After Mom returned home from California, she continued to rehearse the show she was preparing, but on many nights I saw her talking on the phone. She seemed to be very worried. I didn't know what was wrong, but I felt concerned.

Our mom, Michelle, would soon learn that her mother was seriously ill. It was something called "cancer." Shortly after learning this, Mom went to *The Judy Garland Festival* in Minnesota to do the show she had been rehearsing with the little girl. When she came back, she had a huge bouquet of flowers. I know it had been a really big event; something that meant a lot to her, but there was no time to linger over it.

As soon as Mom got back, she told me that she was going to California, and because the trip would be lengthy, I was going too. After what happened to me during her last trip, she didn't think I should be left behind. I know everyone had thought my screams at Theo's approach were exaggerated, but my split ear proved they were not.

I was happy to go to California and live away from the Blossom and Theo for a while. During the day, Mom took care of her mother and checked in on me from time to time. After a while, she got a job so she could make some money. I guess her mom didn't need her help all the time. Her mother, Marian, had always wanted Mom to move back to California, which would have been alright with me, but Mom had always said she didn't want to move. Now that her mother was so sick, she didn't seem to want to be anywhere but California. She was very nervous about her mother's illness.

As usual, at night I slept on the pillow next to Mom. In the middle of the night, she often put her hand on me, and we would play the counting game, tapping back and forth. I knew it was a hard time for her, and I tried my best to help her feel better.

When I needed to, I moved to the bed next to the window to sleep. In the daytime, I would go into the living room and sit on the big corner window seat, looking at the view and sunning myself. I really did prefer this quiet, sunny California life.

After a month and a half in California, Mom said she had to go back to New Jersey to take care of Blossom and Theo. Since she knew her mom was going to have another surgery in a month and that she would be returning, she asked to leave me there. To tell you the truth, I was happy to know I didn't have to get in that little cage and travel again. When Mom showed me my cage, I hissed to let her know I didn't want to go anywhere. I guess she was just testing me.

Mom's brother, Matthew, took care of me while she was gone. He saw that I was fed and that my toilet box was cleaned. Though I did miss my mom during the months she was away, I felt quite at home in West Covina. A lot of her things were there, and I could smell her scent. Still, it was very lonely.

Before she left, Mom asked me to take care of her mom while she was away. So, each morning, when Marian came into the living room to pray, I joined her. She would kneel down on the floor, leaning on the big, white chair just inside the living room door. I would sit on the seat of the chair and put my arms up on the arm of the chair, in just the same position as Marian. Then, she would pray fervently to God and Jesus, asking that He heal her cancer, and I would purr my prayers and thanks along with her prayers.

It was a comfort for me to see Marian, and hear her prayers to God, who made us all. I hoped that I too was a comfort to her. We were two lonely beings, each lonely in our own way.

Time passed, and in November, Mom came back to California for another month. By now, Marian had had her second surgery. I later learned it was liver surgery, though I didn't know what that meant, except that I'd had liver disease, and I knew it was miserable. Marian was terribly miserable after this surgery, and Mom barely had time for me except when we went to bed each night. I knew I was her one comfort, and she was my one comfort as well. Sometimes, she would cry and hold me, snuggling her face into my fur, and I would purr with happiness that she had found me once again. I hoped my purr would make her feel better.

At the end of November, after almost six months on the West Coast, I went to the doctor, got my health certificate, and flew home to New Jersey with my mother. As I walked through the door of our apartment in Jersey City, Blossom and Theo were quite surprised to see me. My time away had made me stronger and surer of myself. I walked right past them without flinching. Then, I jumped on the table and resumed my old seat with the garden view.

Now that Mom was home and believed her mother to be well on the road to recovery, she went back to practicing her singing and planning the next show she wanted to direct. It was a show about Shirley Temple and the songs she had performed in her films. Mom was making a lot of money on her temp job; so, she could afford to put this show on—not that I know much about that.

To save money, we had some of the rehearsals for the show in our apartment. I remember there was a little boy and a little girl who used to come and practice in our apartment, as well as a lady. All this activity gave us cats something to watch. What a time we had! The children came in, sang, tap-danced and ran their lines.

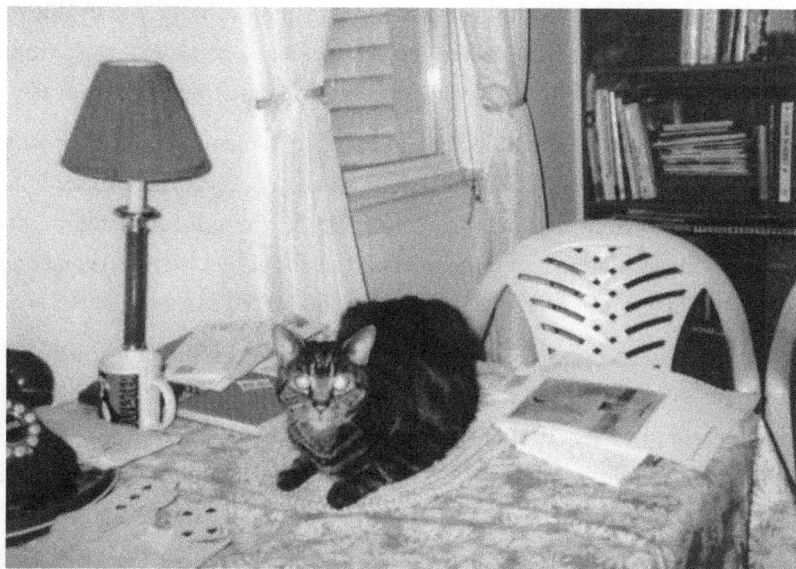

In between rehearsing, the little boy and girl petted and played with us. We enjoyed the children, as well as all the Shirley Temple tapes and movies that Mom played as she studied how to write the show's script. It seemed as if she was always writing and rewriting scripts. Working was her life. She had been in love before and cried a lot. Now, she was happy. And all this entertainment was very interesting for us cats. We were never bored.

The Shirley Temple show went on for a while. Everyone was very excited about it, and we continued to have rehearsals in our home. Mom seemed to be full of joy doing this show, but toward summertime, there were some problems. She cried hard and then closed the show. She said it just had to be done, and that was that.

On the bright side, in the months following her return from California, Mom had grown much closer to her mother. They spoke on the phone every few days and didn't fight anymore. Marian, my "person grandmother," often asked about me, and Mom told her I was fine. It seemed a miracle that Marian was doing so well. She was grateful to have a second chance at life.

Sometime in early summer, our Chinese roommate, Charlie, moved out. Not only had he not made all the money he thought he would make in the stock market, he actually lost money. For several months, he was unable to pay his rent on time. Things were getting worse, and because of this, Mom said he had to go. As sad as the situation was, we didn't regret his move.

After Charlie moved out, Mom had a number of people come up to look at the room. She interviewed the people and had us meet them to see how we interacted. There was one older man, Mr. S, who was interested in the room. Though Marian had some reservations about him based on what our mom told her, Mom Michelle went ahead and rented to him.

About two or three weeks after Mr. S moved in, Mom left us cats with him and went out to California for a vacation. She was feeling very happy and blessed to be able to spend time with her mom. While she was in California, she and her mom rescued a little kitten they found in a parking lot. Marian called the kitten "Baby," and Matthew's dog, Budds, fell in love with it.

While Mom was away, she called Mr. S to see how we were doing. This was something she always did when she was away, but apparently Mr. S took offense to her call. At one point, the landlord came to check on us and see if we were okay. After that I don't know what happened, but one day, Mr. S came into the apartment very upset. He began throwing things into bags and boxes. Then, he opened about six cans of cat food, and put them all over the place. After that, he went down the stairs, banging the wall in fury.

Blossom's fur rose at this display, and I hid in my usual place. We didn't know what to make of it. Following the final bang of Mr. S's slammed door, there was a long silence. It was a silence that went on day and night for several days. It was frightening. We began to wonder if anyone was coming back for us ever again.

Just about the time we began to despair, our mom showed up. It was a good thing too, as we basically had no food left. The food that was left in the cans stunk and had moving creatures in it. I think they are called maggots. It was awful.

That day, when we heard Mom's footsteps in the hall and her cries of horror as she found our food, it took us a little while to come out—we all felt so traumatized. I think Blossom, who was always the most vocal about food, was the first to venture out. Seeing our mom standing there after all we had experienced felt like a dream. We had been alone, in the silence of the apartment for so long, we felt dazed. Mom told us we looked at her as if we were seeing a ghost.

Although hungry, I was fine after this situation, as was Theo, but poor Blossom got a horrible infection on her face. Mom said the vet called it "cat acne." It looked like dark spots, and then it would burst out all bloody, leaving a hole in her face. It took Blossom over a year to recover from this infection.

After Mom's return from California, she continued her regular schedule of work along with singing several nights a week in New York City. Her singing had improved greatly since the time she began getting her voice back in Washington, D.C., and we cats truly enjoyed the times she sang at home. It was like a gift to us. We would all sit together peacefully, listening to her and smiling at the wonderful sounds she made.

That fall, I was not feeling well, so Mom took me to the Chelsea Dog and Cat Hospital in New York City. We had visited this vet before. The trip there was a bit of a pain, though it really only took about twenty minutes. I guess Mom liked to go to old familiar places. The doctor thought I had some sort of upper respiratory infection. With medication and time, it seemed to clear up.

Blossom also made a visit to the vet later in the fall as her face was becoming increasingly infected. She had always been so beautiful. Now, the lower part of her jaw was dark with acne and scabs. Mom discovered that in order to keep the acne from eating away at Blossom's face, it was necessary to try to take the blackheads out every few days. Poor Blossom. She was very patient while Mom worked on her, but it hurt, and sometimes she would scream. Mom told her, "Blossom, please! If I don't do this, your face will be eaten away."

So, Blossom learned to be brave. She knew Mom had her best interest at heart.

Chapter 15
Difficult Days—
The Blessing & The Sorrow

S oon the cold weather returned, and it was Christmas time. Mom packed her things and joyfully left us to go out to California for a week. Everyone was celebrating because Marian was doing so much better. She had finally recovered from her horrible surgery and was continuing to receive a good report from her doctor each month.

When Mom came back from California, however, I noticed right away that something had changed. As the days went by, she seemed distracted and more worried than I had ever seen her. Many nights, she sat on the floor, her back against the bed, talking to her mother, while I sat on the bed above her, listening. After believing her cancer was cured, Marian had just been told it was fatal.

How many nights I sat there listening to Mom as she talked to people, trying to figure out what her mom could do. The doctor had told Marian she was "a dead woman," but as you know, my mom never settled for just one opinion.

During these days, I heard my mom cry as I'd never heard her cry, and I saw the worry. At night, we slept close together. I knew that I was her only comfort, the only one with whom she could communicate without words. Along with God, I was the one who made her feel safe to fall asleep.

By late January, Mom began making plans to rent her share of our New Jersey apartment. As she packed everything in the drawers and took everything off the shelves, putting her belongings in boxes that went up in the attic and into the spare closet, we cats began to get anxious. Mom Michelle even took the pictures off the walls. I, along with Blossom and Theo, wondered what in the world was about to happen. Theo, afraid of losing Mom, tried to crawl into one of her suitcases.

Apparently, Marian did not want all of us cats to come to the house in California. However, Mom was not going to leave us behind. She knew this would be a long visit. Whatever happened, she had had enough of going back and forth—she wanted to be in California with her mother.

Of course, Blossom and I had traveled before. Theo, however, had not. I imagine this trip was a terrifying event for him. He had always traveled in the same cage with Blossom. This time, he had to go by himself. Carrying all three of us to the gate was not going to be possible either. The one thing Mom did for us this time was book a non-stop flight. That way, we would not have to go up and down more than once, and she wouldn't have to worry about any of us getting lost.

I was the only one who got to go inside the plane with Mom, rather than in the dark hole. Just the same, as the engine went on and I heard the rumble of the wheels on the runway, I could not help but cry. In those moments of terror and desperation, Mom leaned over, put her finger in the cage and talked to me. I was still afraid, but at least I knew she was there. Meanwhile, we could hear Blossom screaming from below. Poor Blossom. She did have a hard time.

Matthew, Michelle's brother, picked us up at Los Angeles Airport and drove us to West Covina. I was happy to find myself back in the house there. I knew very well where I was. Soon, Blossom and Theo joined me, spending their days sunning themselves on the single bed close to the window. Even on these winter days, it was warm and bright. At night, we all slept with Mom on the bed away from the window. Somehow during this very difficult time, we cats called a truce and lived peacefully together in a small space. Mom didn't have to worry about us.

Shortly after our arrival, Mom's brother, John showed up with a present for us. It was a big, tall, white carpeted scratching post; about twice the size of my old one. Wow! I guess that was something Mom told him we couldn't live without. It sure was a nice present.

From here on, Mom was busy taking care of her mother, who had just had another surgery. The first weeks after our arrival Marian seemed to be on the road to recovery. Mom checked in with us several times a day, but usually she was in another part of the house for most of the day and evening. When she was not in the other rooms, she was out shopping, taking her mother for treatment, or whatever else needed to be done.

A couple of times, Mom took Blossom to get some treatment for her face. Blossom had taken some medicine, which burned her skin, and now she had no fur on the bottom half of her face. It was all black and pink and scaly. Poor Blossom, who had been so beautiful, looked a sight. I can only imagine how she felt. The new vet gave her some antibiotics and told Mom only to wash her face, and not to use any more topical cream on it. In time, this turned out to be very good advice. Over the next few months, Blossom began to heal and look like her beautiful self again.

The first months in California seemed to fly by. Mom says we arrived on February 16th, 1999. After our first few weeks there, judging from Mom's reaction and the energy in the house, it seemed that things were not getting better for Marian. I no longer saw her in the living room saying her prayers, and she had no interest in seeing me. She was very thin, weak, and tired; a pale remnant of the woman I had been with the year before—and that woman was already very thin.

Then came the night when all the family gathered in the house. It was in April. Marian had been away for a week, and when she came back, they brought her in by ambulance on a stretcher and put her in a special bed with a pumping, hissing machine. The sound of that machine rather frightened us cats. We weren't sure what was going on. We just knew it wasn't natural. Mom fed us, but other than that, she was running back and forth from her mother's room to the kitchen and then talking on the phone. Every time she left the room, we would hear Marian's voice calling her to come back. She didn't want to be alone.

Some of the time, the door to our room was left open. Everyone seemed distracted and no one seemed to worry about us running out of the room. We didn't. We just sat on Mom's bed and stared across the hall into Marian's room. I don't remember where Theo was during this time, but I do remember that Blossom was sitting on the pillow next to me, staring straight ahead.

Mom's brother, John, and sister-in-law, Suzie, came that night and read the Bible to Marian. All the verses were about heaven. During this time, the door to our room remained open, so we could see and hear everything.

Later, Mom told people that as the evening progressed, she felt the room transform. She took her shoes off and could not walk there. It was like the song we had been listening to, "We Are Standing on Holy Ground." Mom said she felt angels were present that night. Blossom and I would attest to that. Cats are not limited to earthly vision, so you can only guess what we saw. Our eyes were wide with wonder—glued to the open doorway of Marian's bedroom. I think for a brief moment, our mother saw us, but then she was too distracted with her own feelings.

Marian left us that night, and a wind blew through the house at that moment. Later, two men came and took her body away. Mom was in the other room, crying and then talking to her step-dad, Ralph. After that, she made a call to her dear friend, Marie. By then, it was nearly morning, and we cats were sound asleep. I only heard later what happened.

Mom said she lay down next to me. I was asleep on my pillow. Just as she was about to fall asleep, our mom felt someone blow into her ear. She jumped up in the bed and turned the light on. She looked at me and nudged me, but I barely moved. I was so tired; I had fallen into a deep sleep. Then, she looked at Blossom and Theo. They were also sound asleep at the foot of the bed. With that, Mom turned the light out, ready to fall into an exhausted sleep. Then, swirling above us were sounds of a distant voice . . . I will say no more.

$$ \text{🐈} $$

In the days, weeks and months following Marian's passing to the next life, Mom and I led parallel lives. We cats had our suite, and there we stayed. On occasion, the sliding door between the dressing room, hall and living room was opened, and we could go out and stretch our legs a bit more. The rest of the time, we just slept on the bed in the sun.

Mom spent most of her time in the kitchen and family room. Her step-dad, Ralph, showed her how to take care of the family business. He and Marian had been a team, and there was really too much work for one person. So, Mom took over her mother's job as best she could. Of course, being in the house, she stopped in to see us periodically, but I know her mind was far away.

From time to time, we also would go down to the house at Corona Del Mar, which was near the ocean. The air smelled so clean and fresh there, and the sun was warm without being hot. We cats loved it, but we were not allowed to go outside. Unbeknownst to us, a neighbor had killed one of Grandmother Marian's cats, Polly's son, Alvin, and Mom was taking no chances. Even so, there were plenty of rooms and windows in this house, and we were still able to enjoy the benefits of being at the beach inside.

Late in the summer, we stayed at the Corona Del Mar house with Mom's brother, Michael, for a few weeks. While we were there, Mom and Michael painted the house and did lots of other work, fixing it up to be rented.

Around this same time, Mom took me by myself to visit her good friend, Alice. We traveled in Alice's car to a place called Malibu and visited some of the places Mom had lived when she was a child. Then, we went to stay at Alice's little house not far from the beach. I enjoyed my visit with Alice. She seemed to know how to communicate with cats. Mom and I were there a few days, and I made myself right at home. By now I had done so much traveling, I knew the routine. It was nice Mom took me with her because I always enjoyed getting out to new places on my own.

I kept thinking maybe we would stay in California. I liked the Corona Del Mar house and felt very much at home in the West Covina house. Altogether, I had spent over a year and a half in that home. But this was not to be. In December, Mom told us we would soon be returning to New Jersey.

Not long before we were to leave, Mom got very sick. She came in one day and got into bed. She said her head hurt terribly, and she lay in the bed for three days barely able to move. Luckily, she had our food in the dressing room, or I don't think we would have been fed. During these three days, we all sat around Mom, watching over her and trying to urge her, or at least comfort her, but she did not respond to us at all.

The first night she shook with chills as she burned under the covers. She had put every cover in the room on her bed, but still she complained she was cold. Her shakes reminded me of the way I felt when I had liver disease. I sat on my pillow and kept my face close to hers.

"Please don't die, Mom," I said, but she only mumbled and was unable even to speak to me. She cried all night long, and once or twice I heard her say, "Who is crying?"

The second morning, she lay there and mumbled, "I have to get up. I have to get up."

It took her a long while to get up, and when she did, she got us some food and put some water by her bed. Then she went back to bed, where she shivered and cried for hours. She kept saying, "I hurt. Oh, I hurt."

I felt so bad for my mom. I wanted to help her, but there was nothing I could do. I simply sat next to her and prayed.

Finally, after two days, she heard Matthew in the hall and was able to find enough strength to get out of bed and go to the door. After that Matthew began to help, bringing Mom medicine, water and juice. Though her fever broke, our mom was seriously ill. Every time she breathed, you could hear the fluid moving in her lungs. When she finally got up, she wheezed and coughed so hard, she nearly fell over. Then she would choke and stamp her feet on the floor, trying to catch her breath.

After coughing hard for days, one morning Mom tried to get out of bed and let out a scream. We cats were so scared; we jumped off the bed and onto the other one, waiting to see what would happen. Mom said it felt like someone had stuck a knife in her ribs. Later, she went to a doctor and was told she had torn her rib muscles.

All this delayed our return east. Marian's husband, Ralph, kept saying, "Are you sure you want to go?"

Mom felt bad, but she knew she needed her own life; she could not just live in her mom's place. She said she might move back to California, but for now, it wouldn't work for her to stay. She packed and packed and packed—all the things that were hers and that she didn't want to be lost. Brother Michael said he would go with us and help drive all these things cross-country to New Jersey. Though I didn't understand all this at the time, one thing sounded great to me—no more airplanes!

Chapter 16
The Long Trip Home

The day after Christmas, we set off on our great trip back to the East Coast. Mom and Michael got a big truck and packed all of Mom's things in the back. Michael suggested we cats ride in the back, too, but Mom would not hear of it.

"They are not luggage," she said, "They will ride with us." And we did.

Michael thought we would go to the bathroom in our cages, but I, Sabrina Russell, will have you know that not once in more than a week of traveling over 3,000 miles did we use our cages as a toilet. Mom was prepared with harnesses and leashes to take us out at rest stops and have us use our toilet box in the back of the truck. However, there was no way we were going to go out in public like that. No, we waited, even if it meant ten hours or more, until we had a nice hotel room!

The cab of the truck was rather large with a seat on each side and a big space in the middle. Blossom and Theo rode together in a cage on the floor of the cabin, and I rode in my cage on top of them. They couldn't see anything. I couldn't see much either, but at least I was closer to the light and to Mom. After the beginning of our journey, Michael never heard a sound out of us.

There were times during the journey when I got restless. I would put my paw out of the cage door bars and call to Mom. I felt very nervous about this trip. It had been so nice and secure in the West Covina home. Now that we were traveling into the unknown again, I felt scared. Some of the time, Mom let me come out to sit on her lap. It comforted me to sit with her.

Some of the time I looked out the window, and other times I'd crawl under her jacket and snuggle up against her. I couldn't tell her all I was feeling, but I was upset and I guess I didn't feel so well. She didn't feel so well either. She had a bandage holding her ribs together and two medicines to put on her chest every few hours. Mom knew I was not as strong as I once had been. I was nearly twelve years old now. I suppose many humans would consider me very old, but I was what I was. Anyway, to Mom, I was just her Sabrina.

There had been two sad events in the West Covina house before we left. Shortly after Marian's passing, Baby ran out in the street and was hit by a car. I know Mom felt very sad about this, but she was glad it had not happened before because Marian loved that Baby cat so much. Then, a very short time before we left, Polly, my granddaughter, was also killed on the same street. She had lived nearly ten years in that house. Although I was not directly affected, we cats can sense these things; so I knew. Now, we were journeying away from this home of nearly a year and away from all these memories.

Our first night on the road was spent in a very small, old motel on a one-street town in Arizona. Mom and Michael were able to go out and sit before a warm fire while they ate a steak dinner. We cats were stuck in a dreary motel room. Well, at least we were able to stretch our legs, and Mom did bring us a share of her steak dinner. That was good!

The next morning, we were up very early and back in the truck for a jaunt to see the sun rise over the Grand Canyon. Of course, the view was for people. We cats saw nothing, and apparently, it was very cold out there, about 14 degrees. Cold out there? While we cats waited in the truck, it got colder and colder for us too! The one advantage of riding in the cab while they were driving was we got plenty of heat!

The second day's ride was long, long, long. I heard Mom and Michael talking about the wonderful views, but in New Mexico they nearly got in a fight because they didn't know where they were. Mom kept singing "Route 66," and when we got to Gallup, New Mexico, she insisted on stopping. All we saw in Gallup were Indians and trucks. Anyway, the trip that day was from about 6 AM to 8 PM.

That night in Santa Fe, we settled down in two rooms in a neat, little, adobe motel. Once again, Mom and Michael went out to dinner. We cats didn't care. We were exhausted and happy to lie down in snug beds. The next morning, Mom and Michael were slow to get started. I was happy about that, but then they went sight seeing and left us in the truck for three hours.

Finally, I heard them say we were headed to Colorado. Mom was driving the truck through a pass from New Mexico to Colorado, and my cage was slanted on an angle upward. We were going very slowly, and I could feel the cold of the snow outside the truck. Michael told Mom to "push the pedal to the floor." "I am!" she said. The truck was so heavy; it could barely get over the mountain in the snow.

When we came down on the other side of the mountain pass, everything was sunny and green. That day's trip was a little less long. Mom and Michael decided to set us up in a really neat, little, pine cabin on a mountain in the woods. Apparently, they had relatives to meet there in Boulder, Colorado and some furniture and things to pick up, so, we stayed in our cabin for two nights. Oh, boy, were Blossom, Theo, and I happy! Our view was peaceful and clean. Mom said we just had to make sure not to sit in the window and let anyone know we were there. I think, besides giving myself a good bath, I slept the whole time we were there.

Two days later, we loaded up and headed east to Kansas. That was another long ride, but by now, we cats were getting used to the routine. You get up in the morning, eat breakfast, go to the bathroom, get in the truck, drive a ways, and wait while the humans eat. Then, you nap all day, until finally it's dark, and you are taken into a totally strange place. Then, you go to the bathroom, eat, stretch your legs, watch some TV, walk around some more, and sleep until the morning when it starts all over again.

We passed through Kansas and Missouri. Those humans took some tourist stops, including the arch in St. Louis. Then, we went on to Illinois.

Now, this doesn't mean much to me, but as it turned out, it was New Years Eve and not only New Years Eve, but the centennial. It was going to be the year 2000, and everyone was nervous about something called "Y2K." They were expecting all the lights to go out or something.

My mom and Michael decided the best place to be on this night would be a little town called Springfield in Illinois, where Abe Lincoln had been a lawyer long, long ago. That afternoon, they found us a nice motel, took a nap, and then headed out and were gone for the night. It was great for us cats, because we were only in the car about five hours that day. What a relief! We were tired, and I suspect after this, Mom and Michael were tired as well.

Where in the world we were going, I wondered. I was patient and maybe I knew, but you never know for sure until you arrive.

We had two more nights on the road. One night, we stayed in Eaton, Ohio and then the next night in the Pocono Mountains of Pennsylvania. From there, the truck went down, down, down, out of the mountains, and it wasn't long until we arrived in Jersey City. Thank goodness, we were on familiar ground once more.

While we were gone—with the help of a friend—we had acquired a new roommate—a guy from France. This fellow, Jerome, had bought a futon couch to sit on in the living room, and two little tables as well. That was great. I came upstairs, and after eating and drinking, I settled myself right on the futon. Mom made me sit on a towel so my hair wouldn't get on the black cloth, but that was okay. I was home again, and what a trip it had been!

Sabrina on the Futon

Chapter 17
Home Again

Now that we were home again, I thought things would go back to being as they used to be, but that was not entirely the case. First, our apartment was rearranged and changed in appearance. Besides the furniture Jerome purchased, there was now an antique secretary, a French settee, a small table, some chairs, a bookshelf and many, many boxes. With all this, the apartment was a lot more crowded than it used to be, and a lot more interesting.

The largest change, though, was our Mom. Her illness had sapped her strength and injured her badly. Because of this, she had to rest a great deal. After a night in bed, it would take her a long time to get up. Blossom, who was not very patient about getting fed in the morning, would urge her on, and Mom would try and try to get up. Finally, as she rolled off the edge of the bed, she would scream in pain. I felt bad for her.

Although Mom went back to work a few weeks after our return to New Jersey, she didn't seem like the same person. She didn't sing or work on projects as she used to do. Instead, she spent most of her time at home with us. Not that we minded. I, for one, was glad to have Mom home, but even then she hardly seemed present. Sometimes in the evenings, she would lie on the bed, stroking my fur while she stared off into space.

"Oh, Sabrina," she told me one night, "If it wasn't for you, I would have no reason to live. I am so alone in the world."

Most evenings now, we cats sat out in the living room with Jerome and watched TV. Blossom and Theo generally sat next to Jerome, while I

When we returned from California with all of Mom's stuff, it was difficult
to find a place to sit

perched myself on the back of the futon, above them. Mom put a towel up there for me, and I felt pretty secure in that spot.

Thank goodness Theo and I could be in the same room now without fighting. It did seem as if he had matured somewhat in the last few years. He and Blossom spent most of their time involved with each other; so, I was left alone. Just the same, when Theo passed me, I often hissed at him, just to make sure he knew I had not forgotten his past transgressions. Even now, I don't trust him. Every once in a while, he will reach out with that big paw of his and bat me in the head!

When spring came, Mom seemed to have healed physically, but her period of mourning had only begun. During this time, I witnessed such terrible grief, I cannot even tell you about it. If a cat cried as she did, they would certainly die. Many times, I sat by my mom, licking her hand and try-ing to comfort her. Blossom tried too, but there was no comfort to be had. Without her mother, she felt lost in the world.

When summer came that year, Mom took a series of trips and left us with Jerome. Jerome was a nice, gentle fellow, who liked cats. He missed his cat back home in France; so, we tried to give him as much company and comfort as he gave us. He was definitely our special friend.

Over the next three years, bit by bit, Mom began to heal. She made new friends, and sometimes they visited us. We always liked having company. During this time, Mom also began to sing again, which meant that she practiced for us cats. Blossom, Theo, and I sat together on the bed facing her, while she sang to us as if we were her audience. Our faces told her how she was doing. Usually, we were pleased, but no loud music or yelling, please!

In addition to Mom's singing, almost every night when we were going to sleep, we listened to a singer named Doris Day. Her voice was so gentle and full of feeling. I know her singing brought my mom much comfort and healing during this time. We cats really liked her too.

Of course, as I've said before, Nancy LaMott was my favorite singer. Shortly before Nancy passed away, she recorded a new CD called *Listen to My Heart*. Mom played this recording almost every day, and I would smile and purr as soon as I heard Nancy's wonderful voice singing those songs. Listening to Nancy was like extra sunshine in my life.

Chapter 18
Health Issues

During the first year back from California, my health was pretty good. I had gained a lot of strength living in the warm sunshine and peace of West Covina. The fact that I was not spending all my time hiding under a bed in the darkness may have helped as well.

Then, a little over a year after our return, in the spring of 2001, I started to feel the old scratchiness in my throat and the crackly feeling in my chest. I always purred at night when Mom came to bed, and she even commented on the fact that my purr sounded odd.

At the time, I didn't know what was wrong or what to do about it. Not feeling well, my mood changed, and some of the time, I became quite nasty. I wanted to hide where no one could find me. Mom told me I was NOT allowed to hide in the back corner under the bed. That really got me mad. I remember hissing and screaming at her when she made me get out.

"Sabrina, it's not good for your breathing!" she told me.

Well, I didn't care, but it was no use fighting Mom. So, I settled on my pillow on the inside corner of the bed and did as she said. Though I was mad at her for forcing me to do something I didn't want to do, I knew she was concerned about me. Soon after that she told me, "Sabrina, I heard about a vet in New York that only treats cats. It's called "The Cat Practice." Come on. Get in your cage! We're going to New York."

Well, did I have a choice?

So after a year of just staying home, we were off on that bumpy train to the big city. Being out of the apartment in the fresh air and sunshine perked me up. It was interesting to see all those cars with the honking horns and the scores of people rushing by.

The people at The Cat Practice were very nice. A man carried me in the back and took what he called an "x-ray" of my chest. When he took me back to Mom, I heard him say, "Oh, she is a beautiful cat! Amazing!"

In a little while, a doctor in a white coat came out. He led us around the corner and had me sit on a cold metal table where he put something on my chest and listened. Then, he told Mom, "Your cat has severe asthma. Unfortunately, it's a very common problem for cats in the New York area. We can control it with medicine, but eventually, her lungs will scar, and at some point, she won't be able to breathe anymore."

It didn't sound very good. The doctor prescribed quite a few drugs for me including Theodur, Azium, Lasix, and a couple other things. Mom paid the bill, put the medicine in her purse, and took me home.

I guess she took the prognosis with a grain of salt. Mom almost never despaired over problems. She always believed that if she looked hard enough, there would be a solution.

Taking six pills or so a day, I became an excellent pill-taker. For a while, the medicine made me feel a little better. It also made me extremely hungry and very, very thirsty. I just couldn't get enough water.

In addition to all the medication, the doctor had given Mom a lot of information, including instructions to count my breaths while I was sleeping to see if I was okay. This was kind of annoying because it seemed as if every time I was just about to doze off, there was Mom, leaning over me, counting my breaths. Of course, she woke me up!

Now, you would think with all that medicine and advice, I'd soon be feeling well. However, less than two weeks after my visit to The Cat Practice, Mom came home one day to find me squatting on the floor at the foot of the bed. My body was tight and stiff, and I couldn't seem to catch my breath.

Desperate, Mom called a cab and rushed me to The Animal Clinic of Jersey City. The vet we saw there was a very nice lady, but after examining me, she said with compassion in her voice, "You know she could drop dead any time."

"I know that," said Mom, stroking my back, but I didn't think she believed it.

I was fourteen years old, but I looked good. I thought of myself as young, and everyone else did too. Mom said she had never had a cat that long, though she had known cats in California who lived to be thirty. Besides that, I had already come back from the dead once.

The vet gave me two shots—one to help my breathing and one antibiotic, as well as some medicine to take home. At home that night, I started to feel better than I had in quite a while. I got up, ate and cleaned myself. The next day, we went back, and the vet took some blood tests. The tests showed that I was a healthy eight-pound cat! The shot they gave me was supposed to last for a while and it did. I continued to feel well for the next four months.

I went back to the Animal Clinic of Jersey City in July to get my travel certificate, and Mom and I flew out to California. I was glad to be in West Covina once again. It was a nice visit and seemed to give my health a boost.

🐈

In the fall of 2001, Mom went back to work for one week. The week after that, she was out of work again and complaining about it. The next day was a Tuesday, and on that day an event occurred which changed everything.

It was a glorious September morning, and I was going about my usual routine. I got up, jumped on the table and vigorously scratched the straw place mat for exercise. Then, I jumped over to the side table in front of the window, where I enjoyed the morning sun and the lively action of all the birds in the big tree outside. While I was sitting there, waiting for my breakfast, the phone on the counter rang.

"Hello, Marie," I heard Mom say, as she answered it. "How are you? What's the matter? No, I didn't go to work today."

I could tell from her voice that something had changed. Mom turned on the TV and told Marie that she saw "it." They were talking about a plane crashing into the World Trade Center. Mom looked out the window where I was sitting, and then out the window on the other side.

"I can't see it," she said to Marie, sounding desperate, "But I see smoke; big, white, puffs of smoke. It's a lot. Oh, my God!" Mom started to cry.

I don't even remember if we got fed that morning or not. I just remember seeing my mom hang up the phone, throw on some clothes, and run out the door. A little while later, she returned and I heard her bolt the inside door. That was unusual. Then, she went into the kitchen and began filling jugs, pots and pans with water. All this seemed very strange. I wondered what was going on.

Mom came into the living room and turned on the television. She sat on the edge of the futon, and she stayed there the entire day. The voices coming from the television seemed desperate and sorrowful, and every now and then, I would hear my mom cry out, "Oh, my God!" Blossom, Theo and I walked quietly around the apartment, sensing fear in the air.

In the evening, the phone rang and Mom ran to pick it up. I heard her say, "Please call my family and tell them I'm alive. The phone lines are full, and I can't make any calls."

Jerome did not come home that night. The city had fallen silent, quieter than it had ever been. Mom lay on the sofa and cried as if her mother had died all over again. We cats sat silently, grouped around Mom as she watched TV, trying to comprehend what was going on. We couldn't understand, but we could feel the terrible tension and grief in the air.

The next day, when Jerome came home, Mom was so happy. She said she was going to the city. She wanted to try to help the people there. Later, she returned because, she said, there were thousands lined up to help.

A few days later, the wind outside changed, and the terrible smell of smoke and ash blew our way. Mom closed all the windows and turned on the air conditioning. She kept checking on me to see if I was okay, but at that point, I felt fine.

The air was filled with tragedy for months after this. We knew something had changed forever. Somewhere out there, it seemed as if the world had stopped. Later, I would hear this day referred to as "9/11." And when winter came and all the leaves had fallen from the trees, the two tall towers that I had often seen twinkling in the dark of night were gone.

⸏

Shortly before 9/11, Mom had begun a new music project. In the days following this terrible tragedy, I heard her asking her friends if she should continue with the project. It was decided that she should. Now, once again, the phone was ringing, and Mom was busy writing and listening to music. We even had a bunch of little girls come to our apartment to sing and try out for parts. This time, Mom told us, "You cats don't need to be in here," so we had to stay in the bedroom. The only one who really complained about that was Theo. He always felt he had to be in on everything.

When November came, I began to have the same wheezing congestion I'd had the prior spring. Mom said she was worried we might have World Trade Center dust in our apartment; so, she went out and rented a carpet cleaner. She did find a lot of dust in our place, and it wasn't dirt.

After that, Mom and I went to the Animal Clinic of Jersey City, and I got an injection of antibiotics and something for my allergies. By the end of the month, I was feeling pretty good.

During the next couple of years, Mom would receive a lot of advice about how to treat my asthma. Some said my asthma might be caused by allergies, and my immune system needed boosting, while others said it might be related to my emotions.

Mom didn't believe I should take too many drugs. Though they helped short-term, she felt that long-term they would weaken me. Because of this, she was always looking for alternatives. The first thing she did was to get me some liquid vitamins. These did seem to boost my health.

Our friend, Kiran, who was a reflexologist, advised Mom that she should work on my meridians. For those who don't know about Eastern Medicine, meridians are the pathways in our bodies that bring energy to all our organs. I didn't really know about it myself, but I soon felt the effects of having my meridians treated. As it turned out, I was really lucky because my mom had already studied Shiatsu (Japanese acupressure) when we lived in Washington, D.C. The only thing she needed to learn was where the meridians are in cats.

To be honest, at first I wasn't so gung-ho about this treatment, but over time, I found that when I was having a really bad asthma attack, Mom was able to prevent me from stiffening up the way I had that day she found me on the floor. As wheezy as I might be, with Mom's help, at least I could still breathe.

Kiran worked on Mom's feet to show her where and how to press my feet. Now, if you know anything about cats, you know we do not like our feet touched. Mom learned pretty quickly that once she pressed a central point in my foot, she had better move fast, or I would get her! I knew she wanted the best for me, but going along with her had its limits. Over time, we were able to work out a compromise.

There was another person who suggested that eucalyptus oil and steam might be good for my lungs. After hearing this, every night Mom started taking me in the bathroom. She ran a hot shower and put some eucalyptus oil in the tub. Our bathroom was almost completely tiled, and with the boiling water running out of the shower spout, the room quickly filled with steam. For a while, I had to stay in that steamy bathroom at least a half an hour almost every night.

This treatment had its limits for me. A lot of times, the bathroom was so hot and steamy I couldn't wait to get out of there. I would scratch the door and say, "Let me out!" Of course, Mom was tough, so I had to stay in the bathroom until my lungs were well steamed. Then, after running the steamy shower, Mom cooled the water down and used it to take a bath.

Over time, Mom stopped running the steamy showers and using eucalyptus oil (which some say can irritate a cat's lungs), but my presence in the bathroom became something of a nightly ritual. It is a ritual I enjoy and look forward to even now. Bath time is a time of day when I can walk around, eat, use my box, and do whatever I want without worrying that any other cat will interrupt me. It's just Mom and me. In fact, while Mom bathes in water, I often give myself a cat bath.

There was another piece of advice we got at this time that Mom has continued to use to this day. A vet told her that whenever I showed any signs of asthma, she should take me outside into the fresh air. Even if the air was cold, he said, fresh air would be the best thing for me.

This suggestion led Mom to wonder if there was a problem with the carpeting or something else in our apartment. Because of this, she bought some rugs to put over the old carpeting. When she went out on warm days, she now insisted I stay in the living room with the windows open, while Blossom and Theo stayed in the bedroom. The living room got all the sunshine and breezes from the river.

Mom also started taking me outside. She would put me in her purse and walk up and down the block, with my head peeking over the top. Other times, she let me wander a bit in the tiny front garden. This was great for me. I enjoyed my freedom out in the fresh air, where I didn't have to worry about being jumped by another cat. I also enjoyed the sights. It piqued my curiosity.

In July of 2002, Mom had to go to California for a while. Hoping the trip would be good for me, once again she took me along. At first, I was really happy to be back in West Covina, but I soon discovered everything had changed. To begin with, the old furniture in our room had been replaced by new furniture with a very strong odor. Right away, my allergies started up. There was also another smell in the room that I found extremely irritating. Mom said it was cigarette smoke, and she began sneezing too.

When daylight came, I thought I might be able to go into the living room and sit in the sun as I used to do in the old days, but upon entering the room, I found everything in upheaval. In fact, the entire house was being taken apart, packed up, and moved out. It was very sad and upsetting to see this. Once again, I started wheezing.

After about a week, Mom said we were going to visit her Dad and step-mom, Christine, in Lake Elsinore. By then, I was not feeling at all well. Aside from asthma, I had also developed the same cat acne Blossom had. Every day, Mom wrapped me in a towel and attempted to clean and remove some of the blackheads from my chin. The treatment saved me from having a year of painful acne, but these procedures weren't pleasant. As a result, I became extremely cranky. I was angry with Mom and the entire world.

At Grand-dad and Christine's house, we stayed in a nice room, but while we were there, my asthma and cat acne were making me miserable. For the entire visit, I stayed in the bedroom in a really nasty mood.

Apparently, during this visit, there were some conversations about me. Mom's dad told her that when he got bad allergies, he'd run a bath with Epsom salts and dunk himself in it.

That night, when Mom was taking her bath, she took me in the bathroom as usual. Then, after she was finished bathing, she threw me in the Epsom salt bath.

"I'm sorry, Sabrina," she said. "I just want you to feel better."

I was absolutely incensed! "Are you nuts?" I thought. "You get me all wet in the middle of the night and think I'll feel better?"

Well, I guess it did help some because the next day I wasn't wheezing anymore, and I began to feel a little more like myself. But please, don't throw your cats into an Epsom salt bath!

Soon, it was time for us to go back to New Jersey, to which I said, "Thank goodness!" Of course, I would have stayed in West Covina the way it used to be, if I could, but now, I was glad to go home. I told Mom, "Please Mom, no more plane trips!" I was knocked out.

Chapter 19

My White Haven, My Home

During 2002 and 2003, life was more relaxed. Mom spent most of her time at home, doing whatever it is humans do. A lot of her time was spent tap, tap, tapping on that computer of hers and staring at the screen. Sometimes, to get her attention, I would climb up on the table where the screen was and sit next to it. If that didn't work, I would sit on the monitor and dangle my tail down in front of the screen, or walk across the keys. That would really get her attention! Sometimes, I sat on her lap while she worked, but most of the time, I stayed across the room on the inside corner of the bed, lying on my pillow. There was a spotlight shining down on me, and I felt quite content there, watching Mom at work.

Mom said she liked working at home, where she could keep an eye on me and see how I was feeling. When she did leave the house, it seemed to be because she was performing in shows, and that made her happy too.

During this time, Jerome moved back to France, and for a short period, several different roommates stayed with us. After that, we had a nice fellow move in who worked long hours. He only came home to sleep; so, we hardly ever saw him. It seemed as if the apartment was just ours, quiet and peaceful, and we liked it that way.

Then, one day in the fall of 2002, Mom put us cats in our cages, took us down to a car, and drove up into the mountains. It was cold there, and there was a lot of snow. When the car stopped, we were carried down a rocky path and up some wooden stairs into a big, beautiful two-story house.

The house was full of furniture, as if someone already lived there. I looked questioningly at Mom. "This is your house, Sabrina," she told me. I looked around and found the house was quite elegant. I decided that I was totally pleased with it. Blossom and I went upstairs and found two bedrooms. We each chose a room for ourselves and settled on a bed. Downstairs, Mom made a fire in the fireplace and sat on the sofa, watching television. This was a real adventure.

In the morning, when I was able to look out the glass wall of windows, I saw how truly beautiful it was. From the back of the living room sofa, I was able to sun myself and enjoy a view of mountains and woods. I decided that I loved this house.

The second day we were there, I had the oddest experience. It was just about dawn when Mom got out of the huge bed we had downstairs and opened the window shade. I was sitting on the bed, looking out, when suddenly I saw something that caught my eye. It wasn't a dog. I had seen dogs before. It was something wild. What was it?

"That's a deer, Sabrina. Do you see it?" Mom asked.

Yes, I did, and I can't tell you the excitement I felt at seeing a wild animal. I was bouncing up and down on the bed looking at this deer, my blood coursing with excitement through my veins. It was there, and then it was gone. What a thrill!

We didn't stay long in this house. We would go there for a few days, or a week and then come back to New Jersey. It obviously was not meant to be our home, but it was ours.

Then, in the summer of 2003, Mom began packing some things in the apartment. She even moved some of our furniture out.

"Oh, no, what is this? Are we going to move again?" I wondered.

Theo was all over Mom about it.

A few days after this, we were put in our cages and loaded into a car. It turned out this car was going to be ours, too.

We drove into the mountains again, but this time we went to another place. There was a small house surrounded by lots of land full of trees,

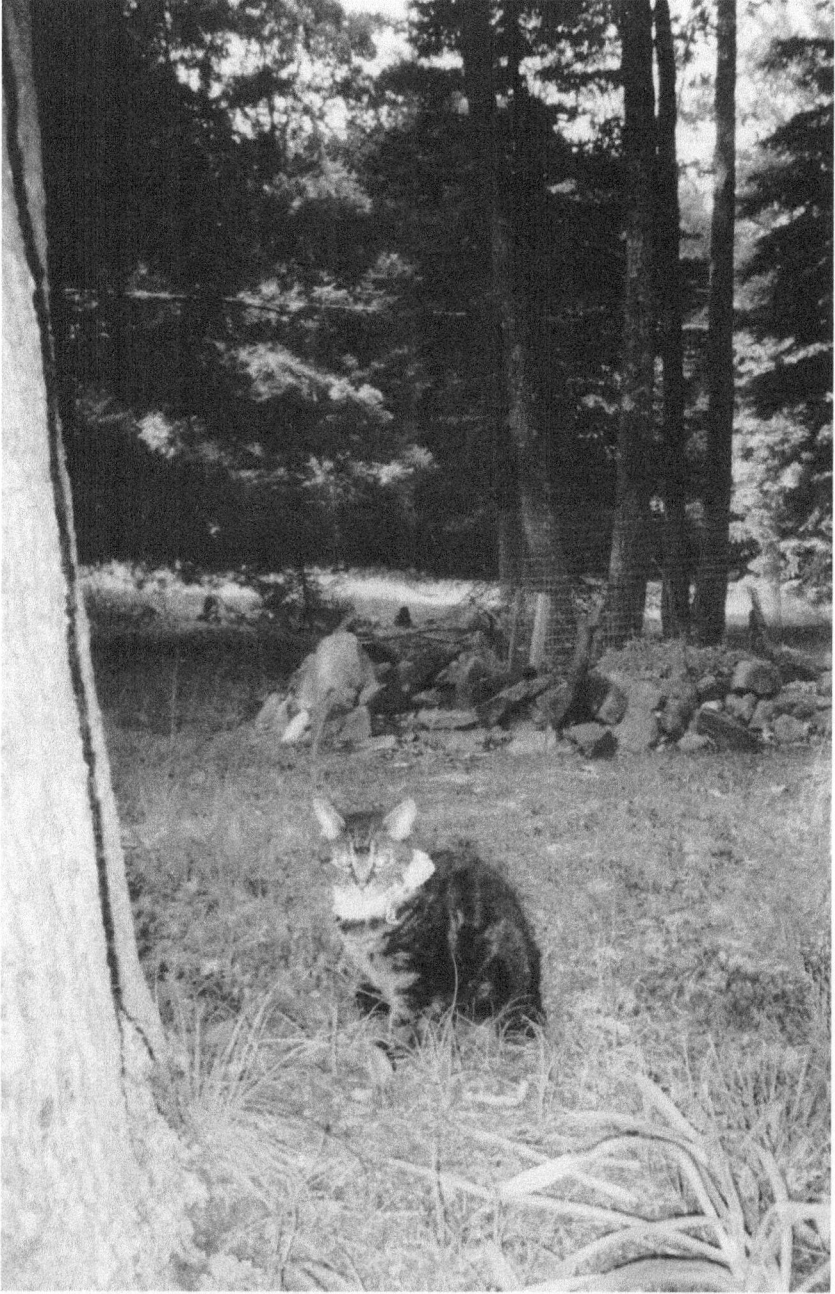

In my beloved White Haven. After I had my neck shaved for a blood test,
Mom gave me a neckerchief to keep the mosquitoes from biting me!

greenery and singing birds. It was cool and peaceful in this place. Mom took us into the house, and we discovered that all the things missing from our New Jersey apartment were there. In the front of the house there was a big window, where we could look out. On the side, there was a big glass door that led to an outdoor room, which overlooked the trees and wild land. We were in the country!

Mom said this was our home—a home away from home. Then, she told me, "This home belongs to you, too, Sabrina!" Well, my goodness!

Because Mom knew she could trust me, I was allowed to go outdoors and roam while she was hanging laundry and doing other things on the property. It was exciting to be free outside. It seemed as if our land went on forever. It was a veritable forest with tall trees, waving ferns and grass. As I roamed around, smelling the evergreen trees and sniffing the bushes, I could smell the scent of the wildlife around me. Unlike Jersey City, there was no street nearby, no noisy cars or people. There was nothing to impede or endanger me in my exploration.

As the days passed and I spent more time outside, I tested the ground by running from one spot to another. I could do it! Every day, I felt a little stronger. Then one day, in great excitement, I ran leaping through the air. I was flying; I was free! My old age, asthma, pain and fear were forgotten. I was young again!

In the distance, I heard Mom calling, "Sabrina! Oh Sabrina!" as she saw me leap unencumbered through the air. I was now seventeen years old. Years had gone by since the doctor had said I might drop dead any moment. No, I was definitely alive. And I was so happy Mom had brought me to this wonderful place! It was my haven.

My favorite seat in the house was the old rocking chair, which Mom had brought from the house in Washington, D.C. It sat in the corner between the fireplace and the big window. Next to it, in front of the window, Mom placed a table with a lamp. This was the spot where I chose to eat my meals. Here, I was able to reach my food easily and, at the same time, enjoy the view. I didn't want to miss a thing.

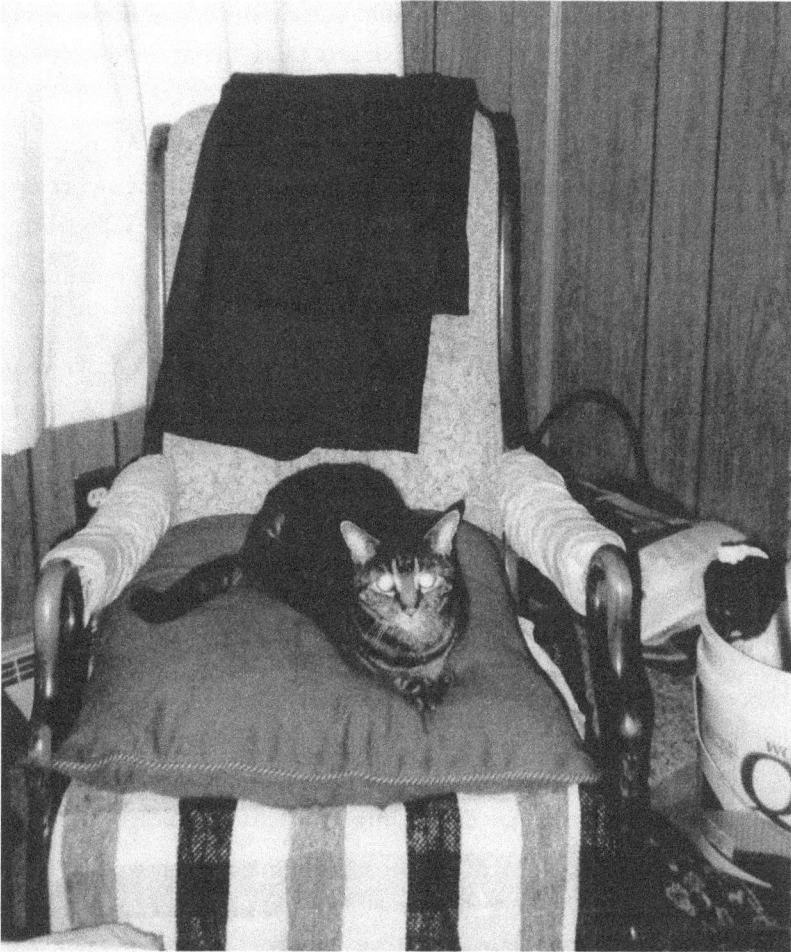

My favorite spot

Those first few days in White Haven (for that was the name of the place), we cats made sure to get up bright and early. The early mornings are when the animals are out. In our yard there were rabbits, raccoons, possums, wild turkeys, chipmunks, and, of course, squirrels. You never knew what you were going to see. Some mornings we even saw mama deer and their babies out munching grass. Our first few days in White Haven, we cats made a huge rumpus in the early morning, as we ran from window to window, trying to watch the animals running around outside our home. Even at night, there were wild things roaming around outside the house. Blossom and Theo were desperate, trying to see what was going on out there. It can get pretty crazy in White Haven at night!

One night, very late, there was a huge bang at the door. At the sound, I rose from my seat with my fur on end. Mom, who was typing on her computer, nearly fell off her chair. Then, in a gruff voice, she said, "Who's there?"

There wasn't any answer. Later, she learned there was only one thing it could have been—a bear!

Because we were living in the wilderness, as soon as it was dusk, we all had to come in the house. Of course, Mom always kept an eye on us anyway. Even now, every time I head down the drive toward the road, my mom will say, "Sabrina, stay out of the road!" Then, I will turn around and come back. She knows I understand her and will listen. Because of this, she trusts me to be out a lot of the time, when the other cats are not allowed out.

During the months in White Haven, we went down to New Jersey just a few times. It seems Mom had rented out our share of the apartment for about six months to see how we liked living in White Haven. It was rather confusing for us cats to find someone staying in our room. Also during this same time, Mom began another project. In August, yes, you guessed it; she packed us up again and took us on a three-day drive to Chicago!

Once we arrived, we shared an apartment with a guy and a girl. It was in the beautiful, old neighborhood of Evanston, just north of Chicago. There were old houses, beautiful lawns, and tall trees. We had our own room with a big row of windows. There was no carpet on the floor and only a bed, a desk and a chair in the room. We also had a fan, which was blowing constantly, as it was pretty hot. Surprisingly enough, the longer we stayed there, the better I felt. In fact, my asthma (which had continued to trouble me, even in White Haven) vanished completely. All the years of ill health and stress had aged me though, and now I was pretty quiet. Most of my time was spent sleeping.

Oddly enough, it was Blossom, who did all the socializing while we were in Chicago. At this point, she was no longer shy and liked to spend her evenings visiting the owners of the apartment and their guests. Mom was out most days, and when she returned, she wrote like mad. I think she was writing a book or something.

We only stayed in Chicago for about six weeks, and then we turned around and went back to Pennsylvania. It was an easy trip home, as we basically knew where we were going.

We were staying in White Haven most of the time now. We watched the leaves change colors and fall to the ground. Nothing unusual occurred during this time. I enjoyed the quiet life and the sights and sounds of the country. I have to say, I had a good life.

Chapter 20
Two Angels

Not long after our return from Chicago, Mom took us down to New Jersey to check on the apartment. Although it was October, the weather was very warm. After about a week of this heat, Mom packed us up again, and we headed back to Pennsylvania.

As usual, I was riding in my cage in the backseat behind Mom, while Blossom and Theo were riding together in their cage on the other side of the car. We had only traveled a short distance when suddenly, I heard Blossom cry out and begin retching horribly. Over and over again, I heard her throwing up. It was awful. Our mother was on the freeway, but she pulled off as quickly as she could, and tried to find a place to park.

By the time the car stopped, Blossom was no longer vomiting, but she had thrown up all over the cage. It smelled awful. Mom cleaned the cage as best she could, pulling the paper out of the bottom and throwing it away. Poor Blossom was shaking from head to tail, while Theo was huddled in the back of the cage trying to avoid the whole thing. Once everything was cleaned, Mom got us back on the road and we continued on to Pennsylvania.

I guess we all thought Blossom's illness had been a momentary event. Elizabeth, her mother, used to have a delicate stomach, and Mom thought Blossom was either suffering from similar problems or else had eaten something bad. She was such a nervous cat. She used to scream at the top of her lungs when Mom was feeding us, as if she thought she'd be left out. For one so shy and retiring, she was really bold when it came to mealtime. Even Theo used to get annoyed and give her a slap now and then.

In the weeks following this episode in the car, Blossom seemed to be very quiet. Mom put our travel futon behind the new sofa, and she and Theo would sit there like they were in their own private living room. Blossom cleaned Theo and took care of him as she always had, and of course, every night, the two of them slept together.

In early November, a few weeks after our return to White Haven, we were all asleep in the big double bed in the front bedroom when there was a sudden and horrible scream in the dark. This was followed by a choking, gurgling sound. Mom sat up and turned on the light.

Theo used to eat plastic bags. A few times, he actually had to be taken to the hospital because of how ill he became as a result. I suppose Mom thought it was Theo choking, but it was not. Theo had jumped off the bed, as had I, and when the light came on, only Blossom was left lying there next to Mom's leg.

I guess Mom thought maybe Blossom was choking because she patted her back, but nothing happened. Then she picked her up, and as she did this, Blossom's entire body just hung there, limp. Mom screamed, and began calling, "Blossom! Blossom! Come on, baby!"

She was patting Blossom on the back, and finally, hung her upside down, as if she had something inside her throat that needed to come out. A little blood came out of Blossom's mouth.

Theo and I left the room at this point. Mom laid Blossom at the end of the bed and then put a towel under her. She was saying, "Oh God! Please help! Blossom! Blossom!"

Over and over again, she cried out Blossom's name. It was a terrible moment, one that Theo and I could not bear to face.

After a while, I guess my mom realized there was nothing she could do. She lifted Blossom in the towel and put her in a box. Then, she put the box in the guest room and closed the door.

By now, the sun was up, and from time to time, Mom would go into the bedroom to look, hoping to see that Blossom had come back to life. Of course, she had not. Theo wanted to go in to see her too, but Mom was afraid

Theo with his beloved Blossom

to let him see her. He was innocent of the whole thing, and Blossom had been there his whole life. She was his heart and soul. He thought certainly Mom would make things right, and she'd be okay. But Blossom was gone.

The next day, when our friend and cat sitter, Lindsay, came over to the house, we were allowed to go in and say goodbye to Blossom's remains. When Theo went in, he turned and walked away with a kind of disgust, as if that was not his Blossom. I looked as well, and then went my way.

I suppose I seemed very cold at the time, and perhaps I didn't care so much. But I was older than Theo, accepting life as it came. Though Blossom and I had shared a life, I kept her outside of mine. My greatest heartbreak had been the loss of my daughter, Elizabeth, and I could not feel more than that. Whatever I felt now, I kept it quietly in my heart. And so, while the others mourned, I went on with my life—eating, sitting on my chair cleaning myself, and looking out the window. I kept my wits about me, but I knew I was living in a terribly sad house.

My mom cried on and on. She said she had not realized Blossom was ill, nor had she realized how much Blossom contributed to our household. Mom said Blossom was the loving one; the one who had made our house a home.

Theo had always been affectionate with Mom, spending most evenings sitting on her lap. He wanted her full devotion. Sometimes, he even seemed to resent any love Mom gave to me. Blossom had never interfered with Theo being in the spotlight. Since she didn't care to have attention on herself, she would sit happily by while Theo got all Mom's attention.

All was changed now. After Blossom was gone, Theo became totally withdrawn. In fact, he showed no emotion at all. He stopped eating. He didn't come into the living room to sit with Mom and me. Instead, he lay on the bed in the spot where Blossom died. When Mom tried to hug him, he turned his head away and lay limply in her arms.

At night, when we came into the bedroom to sleep, Theo went and sat on the futon where he and Blossom had spent their evenings. It seemed very strange to see him walk by and not even notice me. I can't say I was unhappy about this, but it just seemed odd. It was as if he was a different cat.

I could see Mom getting more and more upset as she realized that Theo was fading away. Finally, she started yelling at him. She knew she was going to have to fight to keep him alive. She cried at him, "Don't die, Theo! I love you! We need you here with us! Theo! Theo! Are you listening to me? Come back!"

It was quite clear that without Blossom, Theo had lost the will to live. Our little family had gone everywhere together and lived through so much. Now it was broken and shattered, and it would never be the same again. Then, God sent someone in need to help us.

🐈

It was only few weeks after Blossom's passing, and we had just had a big snow. That day, Mom decided to go over to the Big Boulder house and do some work. The house had been rented for nearly a year, and when the people moved out, they left a terrible mess. Aside from the people, a very nasty cat and a dirty ferret had also been living there. In fact, the place was so dirty, Mom wouldn't even let us cats stay there, and I loved staying in that house. It was one of my favorite places.

Anyway, as the story goes, Mom had been working on cleaning the house, and it was getting dark; so, she started to pack up to come home. Just then, she looked at the glass front door, and there was this skinny, dirty cat looking inside. Since it was freezing cold with a foot of snow outside,

Mom went and opened the door, but the cat got scared and ran away. A few minutes later he was back. This time when Mom opened the door, he came inside. He tried to cry, but he had no voice.

Mom knew the cat needed help; so, she gave him some of our cat food, which luckily was still in the car from our last trip. Then, she left him in the house over night. The next morning, she went back and took him to our vet. After the vet said he was okay, she brought him back to our house, and snuck him into the guest room. I say "snuck" because for weeks, neither Theo nor I had any idea there was another cat in the house! After all, we never used the guest room.

This little cat had been living outside for a while, and though he had a thick coat, he was bone-thin. In fact, he was so thin and exhausted that for almost a month, all he did was eat and sleep. In addition to this, it seems that his nose and his mouth had been burned somehow. The black on his nose was really a scab and when it came off, his nose bled. The vet thought that someone had put a chemical or something on him and tortured him. Even though he didn't have any real illnesses, he was a pretty sick little boy.

His presence in our home was a big secret. In fact, Mom didn't really want to keep this cat at all, especially since he was a boy. I heard her asking a friend to please help her find a home for some cat, but I certainly didn't know the cat was in our house!

Meanwhile, Mom was still battling to get Theo to want to live. Then one day, Theo was walking through the hall when he heard a noise in the guest room. I heard it too. It sounded like scratching. Well, Theo got very excited. I think he thought maybe Blossom, who had been laid out in that room only a few weeks earlier, had come back to life. His ears perked up and he became curious to determine the cause of the noise. At this point, Mom decided to open the door and see if the little cat wanted to come out. So, she did.

This little gray cat with a white front, white paws and a partially white face, walked shyly out of the room. Of course, Theo was very, very disappointed and upset to see it was not his beloved Blossom come back to life. I guess I was too. The first time I saw that cat walk through the living room, I said to myself, "You have got to be kidding! What is this?"

Pennsy

But the little thick-furred cat walked by us as if we didn't even exist. He was not afraid. He really had no interest in us at all. He obviously wanted to stay in our house, so, he was playing it very cool.

Mom told us," This cat has had a very hard time, and he's just visiting—so be nice. Soon, he'll go to another home."

Because he was a boy, I guess Mom didn't think he and Theo would get along. Theo hissed at him a few times and then walked out of the room, but the new cat didn't pay any attention. He sat himself down in front of the fireplace and went about his business.

To be honest, I actually thought he was kind of cute. I didn't want to be bothered with him, but I know Mom caught me smiling to myself as I looked at him. Yes, even at my age, I know a cute cat when I see one!

This cat was not very big, and he seemed very sweet. It was clear he was not at all interested in confrontation; he was only interested in keeping a roof over his head. I heard Mom tell him, "If you want to stay here, you have to get along with the other cats."

The cat adored my Mom. He rubbed up against her and threw himself at her feet. I could see that bit by bit, she was becoming attached to him. How can you send someone away who adores you?

Mom named the cat "Pennsy" for Pennsylvania, and he took to the name right away. Pennsy was very loving, affectionate and sweet. It was hard not to like him, though I made it clear that I didn't want him to get too close. In fact, Mom had to fend him off for a while because he was quite attracted to me! But we soon worked that out. So, it seemed that Pennsy was here to stay.

It also took a while for Theo to accept Pennsy, but eventually, he did. Pennsy, from his appearance, could easily have been the son of Blossom and Theo, and Theo soon adopted him. The two began spending a lot of time together and became best buddies. Although Theo would never completely be his old self again, Pennsy really helped him heal from the loss of his soul mate. Pennsy gave him a reason for living. I think the deal was cinched after Mom saw that Theo and Pennsy really got along.

One more note on Pennsy: One day Mom was sitting on the couch by herself, and I was sitting in my chair by the fireplace. Then, talking to no one in particular Mom said, "You know, cats are angels God sends to help us."

Just then, Mom felt a tap on her shoulder. She had been so lost in thought, not expecting an answer; she practically jumped off the couch. Then, turning to look behind her, she saw Pennsy smiling wisely at her. Mom's eyes got real big, and she said, "Oh, my God!"

I think she had just been talking fancifully, but when she felt the tap and looked into Pennsy's eyes, she got the answer!

Chapter 21
Traveling Days

When winter came, it turned the landscape into a shimmering, white wonderland. We stayed in the mountains for the next four months. Once in a while, we would go over to the newly restored house at Big Boulder to stay, but most of the time, we were in White Haven. It was far too cold for me to play outside now. The closest I got to that was looking out the big picture window while I ate my meals. For Christmas, Mom bought me a soft, warm blanket, and most of my time was spent wrapped up in it, sitting next to the fireplace.

Having seen how I ran and leaped outdoors in the summer, it was hoped that country living would help restore my health. Unfortunately, once winter began, although I wasn't having asthma attacks, my nose was constantly stuffy and wet. At the end of December, Mom took me down to the White Haven Veterinary Hospital in the little town of White Haven. The vet there was located in a big, old house, and they were always very pleasant. While we were there, the doctor and Mom discussed what might be causing my problems and what could be done to solve them. I was somewhat more fragile than I had been, and Mom said she wanted to find a way to make me stronger.

Then, one morning early in January of 2004, Mom said a prayer over me and told me that the doctor was going to try to help me feel better. We went down to the White Haven hospital early that day. I didn't even get any breakfast. When we got there, I knew something was different because Mom didn't wait with me. She just handed me over to a lady and left.

The vet's assistant took me in the back and put me in a cage where I got very sleepy. I don't remember much of anything after that, except for waking up and sitting under a sun lamp. I guess my nose did feel cleaner, but I always felt better out of the house.

When Mom came to pick me up, the vet explained that she had washed out my nasal passages. She had thought I might have some extra gunk in my sinuses, but there didn't seem to be any. She also told Mom that my x-ray showed some kind of a bony protrusion, possibly a tooth, at the back of my nasal passage, but it wasn't something they could remove.

"The best we can do at this point, with her age," the vet told Mom, "is to keep an eye on her and medicate as needed."

When March came, we all moved back to Jersey City. With the exception of visits to White Haven now and then, we would stay in Jersey City for the next six months. That March, when we arrived back in New Jersey, I ran happily up the stairs to our apartment. It was great to return and discover old familiar surroundings. The first thing I did was jump up on the table and look out window to see what was going on outside. It felt good to be home.

As you know, I was now an experienced traveler, but for Pennsy, all this was new. Luckily, he seemed to catch on fast. Before long, he was making himself at home in New Jersey too. No matter where we went, he remained the same sweet cat. I had no problems with him at all.

In April, our old roommate moved out and a new lady from South America, Marta, moved in. We didn't see her too often, but she was very nice and quiet. She practiced Yoga every morning, gave Shiatsu, and had a very, peaceful presence.

The month we returned, I had to go to the doctor in New Jersey for my asthma, but after that, I didn't have any more congestion. Mom continued to study which vitamins to give me and cooked my favorite chicken soup. She also started growing grass in a little pot on the windowsill. Every morning that was the first place I headed. I loved to sit in the window and eat my grass. Life in our Jersey City apartment was most enjoyable and homey for me. Soon summer was in the air, the windows were open, and the fans were constantly blowing. I felt pretty good.

When we were up in White Haven, Mom started taking me out in the car when she went shopping or to church. Since I didn't feel like running the way I used to, I really enjoyed these little rides. They gave my lungs a chance to breathe and, at the same time, let me see things outside without much effort. While we were riding on the highway, I was always in my cage. Once we stopped, if it was cool enough to keep the windows up most of the way, I would be allowed to get out and see where we were. In this way, the spring and summer of 2004 passed quickly.

One day in late summer, while we were down in Jersey City, Mom cleaned all of our personal things out of the bedroom and packed a few more things than usual into the car. With that, she loaded us up and took us back to Pennsylvania. A few days later, we were put back into our cages. This time we didn't go far, only out to the deck while some men tore the old carpet out of our house, replacing it with thick padding and new carpet. When we came back inside, the floor under my feet felt really soft and clean.

"See, Sabrina," Mom said, "Nice, new carpets. I hope that makes you feel better."

Little did we know—later those carpets would be a cause of even greater problems for me.

Chapter 22
To Tennessee and Back

As you may gather, I never knew what Mom was cooking up, but you could always be sure she had something going. So, it was no surprise to us cats when, a few days after our new carpet was installed, she packed the car, put us in our cages and drove off. There was nothing I could do but resign myself to the fact that we were off on another adventure. I was used to it by now.

One thing I forgot to mention was the fact that after Pennsy joined our family, Mom went out and bought him a new cage. It was really a big one and very nice. Unlike our square and somewhat worn and flimsy cages, this cage had a curved top and felt very secure. Mom called it "the Cadillac" of cages.

At that time, Mom didn't know what kind of traveler Pennsy was going to be. It turned out; he was a little like Blossom—a scaredy cat—who screamed all the way. Once Mom saw that he and Theo were going to be "best buddies," she put him in the cage with Theo. That worked great. Theo was really good at calming cats down (everyone, that is, except me!).

Anyway, since Pennsy was riding with Theo, Mom decided to give the new cage to me. Now, instead of being cramped and hot, I was riding in style with lots of room to stretch out and relax. Theo and Pennsy were happy together, and I was happy too.

For the entire three days of our trip, I sat in my cage enjoying the sunny, peaceful ride. From time to time, we stopped along the way, and because Mom knew she could trust me, she'd take me out on a leash and let me walk in the grass. I can now say that besides having eaten grass in Washington, D.C. New Jersey, California and Pennsylvania, I have also eaten grass in Ohio, Kentucky and Tennessee. Altogether, I have visited twenty-two states in my life.

Although this trip was long and tiring, the best thing about it was getting all that fresh air. My lungs really got cleared up on the road, and I didn't have any asthma attacks. I know people are always saying that cats cause asthma. Well, that's not true for me. Aside from seasonal pollen, it's all the carpeting and pollution people make that causes my asthma.

Our two nights on the road were spent in motels. Whenever we arrived at a motel, it was all hush-hush while Mom covered our cages and went into the office to get a room. Then, she'd drive back to where the rooms were, and one by one, sneak us in under a jacket or a sheet. I was easy, and my seniority generally meant that I got to go in and stretch my legs first. Then, Theo was brought in and finally Pennsy.

Sometimes Pennsy had to stay in the bathroom while he calmed his nerves. He wanted desperately to look out the window and see where we were. I knew we weren't supposed to do that, because Mom told us, "No one is supposed to know you're here!"

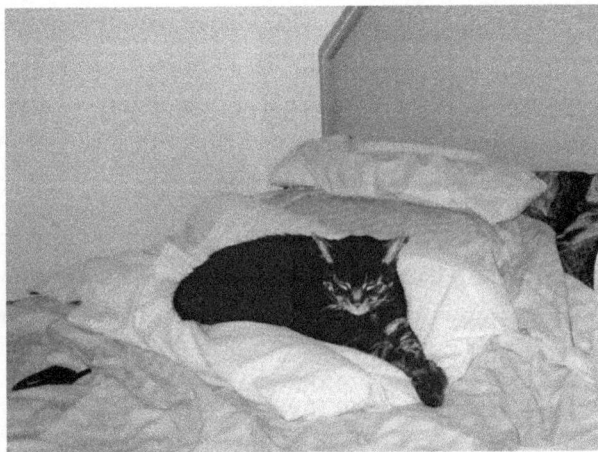

Relaxing in my room at the Knights Inn, Murfreesboro, TN

Once Mom had us safely in our motel room, she would fix our toilet box. Then, we'd have a good meal. The boys would eat on the floor, while I was served on one of the bed stands, where I could take my time.

While we were eating, Mom put a sheet over the bedspread for us and turned on the TV. Then, we'd all make ourselves at home. The boys sat at the foot of the bed in front of the television, while I took my usual spot, on my own pillow at the head of the bed.

We arrived in Murfreesboro, Tennessee, in late September of 2004. At the Knights Inn Motel where we stayed, we didn't have to hide. They were expecting us, and it seemed that we were going to stay there for a while. Mom even set up her computer. That suited me just fine. I was sick of traveling. Our room was at the end of a long line of rooms, and people would come down just to look in the window at us. It was nice and warm in Tennessee, and sometimes Mom would take me out for a walk so I could get some fresh air. The only problem with going outside in Murfreesboro was there were lots of mosquitoes.

A man named C. B. Arnette used to come and take Mom around to look for places to live. With his help, about three weeks after our arrival, Mom found a place. It was on the second floor of a building in a square of apartments. There was a living room, bedroom and bathroom. It was all very clean and quiet. In the daytime, the sun came in the front window, and we cats would all lie on the living room floor, enjoying it. We didn't have any furniture at the time. In fact, our first week in the new apartment, we all slept on the floor with Mom. After that, Mom bought a bed, desk, table, some chairs, and a nice red rug on which we cats liked to lie. That was all the furniture we had in Tennessee.

For the next few months, Mom was out almost every day. At night, she would sit at her desk and work on her computer most of the time. It seemed she was writing a book. That's why we were there. Of course, she would stop her work now and then to check on my breathing.

A lot of the time Mom was working on this book, she played old Tennessee music on our CD player. I did enjoy that old country music with the banjos and singing. It's so lively and pleasant. I actually felt pretty good during this time, though once in a while, my medication needed to be increased.

After we had been in this apartment for a couple of months, Mom went away for about a week, and a nice lady named Aleesha came to take care of us. When Mom returned, she told us we were going to move to a house. It seems she was not happy with the loud noise that came through the walls of the apartment late at night. It irritated her. It was bothersome to us cats too, but not as much as it was to her.

Our new house was in a very old part of town. The house itself was over one hundred years old. It had a flat carpet and a lot of rooms to explore; some were sunny, and some were dark. Mom took me over to see the house one day by myself. I really enjoyed that. The unique thing about this house was that every room had at least two doors, so you could you could walk through the entire house in a circle without going though any door twice.

A week after I visited our new home for the first time, everything in our apartment was packed up and moved there. Our bed was put in the sunny room next to the kitchen. This is where I spent most of my time. The walls were pink, and there was a long window through which the sun shown almost every day. We also had a fireplace with a grand mantle. A large, old, electric heater sat just in front of it. This was the only source of heat in our room, so Theo, Pennsy and I called a truce, and the three of us would sit together before it, enjoying its warmth.

The other door in this room led to the living room where Mom had set up her desk. Just off the living room was the bathroom. Once Theo and Pennsy arrived at the house, we had quite a bit of fun roaming round and round through the rooms in a huge circle. I didn't even bump into the boys once!

Sometimes during the winter days, it was warm enough for Mom and me to sit on the old wooden porch and look out at the lovely street. The street was lined with large, old trees, grass and other pretty homes. Our house was very close to the sidewalk, and often, passersby would greet us as they went on their way. Mom knew she could trust me not to run off while we were sitting on the porch. I only jumped off the porch once in a while so that I could eat grass.

While we were in Tennessee, I started taking a lot more trips in the car. At least once a week, I went on some little local trip. One time, we went to Petsmart (you know, "where the pets go"), and Mom let me sit in her purse while she went inside. I got to look at the guinea pigs and mice. In my old age, not too many things excite me, but that was exciting. I perked right up when I saw those mice!

As we walked around the store, everyone was so surprised to see my face peeking out of Mom's purse. They all asked about me and were amazed to find out I was nearly 18 years old. The outing to Petsmart was a pretty nice trip, but when it was over, I came home and went right to sleep.

During the spring of 2005, Mom took me to see an eye doctor. The vet at the South Church Street Animal Hospital in Murfreesboro had given me some eye drops and suggested to Mom it might be a good idea to get my eyes checked. It seemed as if my sinus trouble might be affecting them. Until that moment, we didn't even know there was such a thing as an ophthalmologist for cats!

The ophthalmologist was in a small town called Nolensville about twenty miles from our home. The doctor's office was in a very old country farmhouse. There were quite a few big dogs coming in as patients, but I didn't see any cats while I was there.

When the doctor came in, he put some drops in my eyes. Then, he turned off all the lights and shined a small light in my eyes. He said my left eye was nearly blind, but he would prescribe some drops so that it wouldn't get any worse.

"I think she may have had an infection or injury of some kind that put pressure on the nerves in her eye," he told Mom. "It's not reversible now, but her other eye is still pretty good."

After our visit, Mom recalled the summer before in White Haven when I spent a lot of time sitting on the sofa. I had had a terrible headache, but how could I tell anyone how bad I really felt? Maybe I needed medicine then, but I didn't know there was a solution for how I was feeling. Mom kept telling me how sorry she was that she hadn't gotten medicine for me at that time. She understood now what had been going on.

The important thing was that I wasn't blind. I could still see to get around in the daylight, just not that well in the dark. Sometimes when I was walking around, I would bump into things if they were on my left, the side of my troubled eye. I often mistook Mom's dark handbag for Theo. I would hiss at it, just in case it was him. There were also a couple of times when I leapt for something and missed, falling down. That was terribly embarrassing for me.

By the end of February, spring had arrived in Tennessee. The grass was green, the flowers were blooming, and the air felt nice and warm. I really did enjoy that warm sun. You know, when you get old, it feels good on your bones!

Unfortunately at this point, Mom said we had to pack up and go back to Pennsylvania. That's another thing about getting old—you don't feel like traveling that much; so, I wasn't very happy hearing this news. This trip back to Pennsylvania was extra long because Mom needed to do some research along the way. We drove all the way down to Rome, Georgia first, where we stayed overnight. Then, we traveled through Atlanta, into South Carolina, North Carolina, and finally, Virginia.

In Virginia, we stopped to meet some people who were associated with the book Mom was writing. It was a nice day when we arrived in Virginia, so Theo, Pennsy and I sat out in the sunshine in our cages, while Mom went

Relaxing in my fancy Virginia hotel room

inside the house to visit. Funny, it was such a nice day, because the next day we got caught in a blizzard!

That day in Virginia, Mom drove until she was too tired to go on. Then, she stopped at a really nice hotel, with a tall, mahogany bed and fancy covers. Mom took a photo of me sitting in the bed like I was a queen. I always knew I was meant to be a ritzy cat, and this place suited me just fine. The only thing was, our hotel room was right across from the main office of this high-class place, and Mom had to do some real sneaky stuff to get us into our room.

The next morning, when we woke up, snow was coming down in fluffy, little flakes. The further north we went, the bigger those snowflakes grew. By the time we reached Washington, D.C., we were in a blizzard. Mom apologized to me, because she knew I would have loved to see my old home on Capitol Hill once more, but she said we just had to push on in this storm. We did push on, and by nightfall, we were safe at home in White Haven. It was spring when we left Tennessee, and the dead of winter only four days later, when we arrived in Pennsylvania!

Chapter 23
My Pennsylvania Vets

As we walked through the door of our White Haven home, the clean, furnished rooms with new carpeting looked beautiful. For six months, we had lived in spare conditions, with very little furniture. Now, our Pennsylvania house felt like a palace. It did not take long after our arrival, however, for my nose to start running, and my lungs to become wheezy.

Neither Mom nor I understood it at the time. We thought our clean, beautiful home would be a healthy respite after our long journey. It was only later we learned that having a newly carpeted home closed up for six months was not a good thing. Apparently, these carpets were giving off toxic fumes, which—with my compromised health—affected me more than anyone. And now, with the sub-freezing temperatures of the Pocono Mountains, it was not the time for Mom to open the windows. I had grown so much stronger and healthier in Tennessee; it was very frustrating to find myself ill again.

There was some relief, though, because one week after our return East, Mom took us back to New Jersey and I began to feel much better. I was so happy when we arrived at our New Jersey home. To keep me from having to work so hard, Mom carried me partway up the stairs. Once I entered the apartment, I jumped to my favorite spot on the sofa and began purring. I was home, and relieved to be there.

The morning after our arrival, I was up in the window, looking out, enjoying the sun. The air in New Jersey was warm enough for Mom to open the windows. This was one place I really felt I could relax, and that is what

At home in Jersey City

I did. Although, I didn't know it at the time, sadly, my happiness there was to be short-lived.

As always, Mom was busy with new plans. Marta, our roommate, was getting ready to leave, and we needed to find another roommate. People were coming and going, looking at the place, and Mom was in and out as well. During this time, I just sat in the window, or lay on the futon, enjoying the warm sunshine and gentle breeze.

For the next few months, we continued to travel back and forth between White Haven and Jersey City. I really didn't understand all that was going on at the time; I just tried to content myself with finding the best in each situation.

During this time, I continued to have quite a bit of congestion. I went to the White Haven Animal Hospital in March, and to the Jersey City Animal Clinic in May. Then, in late June, Mom took me back to White Haven for another check up and some more medicine.

Usually, we saw the same nice lady in White Haven, but this time we saw a new vet, a young man. Besides giving me antibiotics, this young man also prescribed Prednisone. Mom was a little uncertain about this prescription. She gave it to me for a few days, but it didn't seem to affect me well, and I didn't want to take it. After a few days, Mom agreed with me, and decided she wouldn't give me the pills anymore. When she checked her favorite book, Anitra Frazier's *The Natural Cat,* she read that Prednisone can cause kidney failure in cats with as little as one dosage. The next week, when we went back to the White Haven Animal Clinic, I received some different medication. Later, Mom wondered if she made a mistake in allowing this young, inexperienced vet to treat me with Prednisone.

Whenever I had to take medicine, Mom would always tell me, "Come on, Sabrina. Take this so you can be a healthy girl."

I tried to do as Mom said because I always remembered how she helped me get well when I was so sick with liver disease. But there were times, I got tired of taking all those pills, and sometimes they didn't go down right. When this happened, I could taste them and I would start foaming at the mouth. Usually, though, I took them pretty well. Mom would open my mouth and put the pill in from the side. Then, she would close my mouth and scratch me under the chin, saying, "Swallow, swallow!"

After this last bout with allergies, Mom told me, "Sabrina, all these pills are not good for you. Mommy needs to find you a holistic vet to strengthen your immune system, so you can stop taking them." And that is what she did.

On July 1st, Mom put me in the car, and we drove about an hour away to Harvey's Lake Veterinary Clinic. Dr. Buccha, the holistic vet, was a very gentle and nice man. I liked visiting him. He took a lot of time, carefully examining me as he tried to find a solution for my breathing problems. Then, he sent us home with a package of something called *Missing Link* and a bottle labeled *F-Biotic*. These were to add nutrition to my food and strengthen my immune system. In addition, Mom went to the health food store with a list of vitamins Dr. Buccha suggested she buy for me. These included liquid B, C, E and Coenzyme Q-10. I was to take most of these in small quantities every day. This was a lot of work for me, and it took some time to accept all those different flavors going into my mouth.

Only a few days after our visit to Dr. Buccha, Mom took us cats back to New Jersey. While we were in New Jersey, I started feeling much better. In fact, I didn't need any asthma medication for the entire three weeks we were there. This was pretty amazing as it was the first time in more than a year that I had gone even one week without any pills!

The bad thing was, as soon as we got back to White Haven, I started having asthma problems again. After such great success in New Jersey, that was rather distressing. Even worse, was the knowledge we would soon be moving out of our Jersey City apartment and living full-time in White Haven. As much as I loved our White Haven place, Jersey City still felt like my real home. For almost eight years, no matter how many times we went away, we had always come back. I was very sad to see our home taken apart.

The truth, Mom told me, was that she was running out of money, and she hadn't been able to get any of her usual New York work. Maybe she could have gotten a permanent job, so we could have stayed, but by summer, it was evident that we would soon have to return to Tennessee. Sustaining our New Jersey home as well, Mom said, had become too much.

While I didn't understand all this, I saw the results. Bit by bit, the old familiar objects like the tables, futon, and other things began to disappear. Mom sold some of these items, and the rest were moved to White Haven.

As usual, I resigned myself to the fact that Mom had decided what we needed to do. I know she felt bad, but she believed this would be for the best. Despite my ill health and desire to rest, life with Mom was always interesting. It was a constant adventure of new scenery that kept me young.

Chapter 24
Difficult Days

Toward the end of July, as we were preparing to move, something else happened. Suddenly one evening, I didn't feel at all well. I kept trying to go to the bathroom, but very little was coming out. When Mom came into the bathroom with me, she looked down at the brown, tiled floor and saw blood! At that moment, I was feeling very weak; almost dragging myself across the floor. I heard Mom say, "Oh, no, Sabrina!" Then, when she picked me up and saw more blood coming out of me, she started to cry.

By now, it was late at night, but Mom wasted no time. She put me in my cage, and pretty soon we were on a train heading for New York City. Mom let me know she was taking me to an excellent all-night animal hospital on Fifth Avenue. When we came out of the subway, it was almost midnight. It seemed strange to see all the streets and tall buildings so dark and quiet. At the hospital, the doctors took blood and urine from me. Then, they gave me some fluids under my skin, and sent me home. The doctor told Mom it would be a few days before they got the test results and knew how best to treat me. They thought I would be fine until that time. I know Mom was very scared. When we got home, she cried over me and kissed me a lot. I just felt glad she knew something was wrong.

About three days later, Mom went back to the hospital and got my test results. The doctor told her I had an E. coli infection in my bladder and gave her some medicine for me. That was pretty serious, but it was not my only problem. The doctor also told Mom I might have kidney disease, and I should see my regular vet immediately.

The next day, we went to the Animal Clinic of Jersey City. As we entered the clinic we had visited so many times before, I could feel my mother's fear. I wasn't feeling great, but I had never felt more fear in her.

Inside the examining room, the doctor talked to Mom about my condition and told her the situation was not hopeless. Apparently, Mom had thought when a cat got kidney disease, their life was over. The doctor said that I seemed to be in the very early stages, and at this point, my condition could be controlled with fluids and diet. The doctor gave Mom a bag of fluid and some needles and showed her how to put the needle under the skin of my back where it wouldn't hurt. The fluid would pool there and then be absorbed into my body. I was to get these fluids every day to start, and then possibly every few days. We would have to see how much I needed.

The doctor also told Mom there was still a chance that once I recovered from my e-coli infection, my blood levels might return to normal. She said I should come back in a month or so and get re-tested. With this news, Mom perked up. In the past, whenever I'd taken a blood test, my results were always excellent. We just had to hope and pray for the best. So, we went home. I took my medicine and my fluids, and I didn't have any more blood in my urine; I seemed to feel pretty good.

Following the doctor's instructions, each day Mom put a pillow on the kitchen counter and set me on it. The bag of fluids was hanging on the cupboard knob just above me. Then, talking to me all the while, Mom would pull the skin up from the back of my neck and push the needle for the fluids into the tent of skin on my back. She used to apologize to me each time, saying, "Oh, Baby, I'm so sorry. I didn't hurt you, did I?"

We both knew it had to be done, and as time went on, Mom learned to give me this treatment in a way I barely felt. The entire procedure only took a few minutes. With our very busy lives, these few minutes soon became a special time for us. Mom would talk to me, pet me, and massage me. I got a lot of love during those moments. Mom had always taken good care of me, and I trusted her. I knew she would do whatever was needed to make me feel better.

Meanwhile, during this rather traumatic time, there was so much going on. Seeing my much-loved New Jersey apartment slowly emptied was very sad. We had experienced a lot within those walls.

Once we had finished the move to Pennsylvania, I got to go outside a lot. I did enjoy that. Still, the air in the house continued to irritate my lungs. Even Mom was sneezing. In an effort to improve my health, Mom bought a large air filter. She also bought a juicer and started juicing some things for me, though I have to say, while I liked Mom's cooking, I didn't enjoy the green drink she made for me. Neither did I enjoy the carrot and apple drink. That one made me drool! Nevertheless, I accepted a couple of spoonfuls each time, and I guess some of that stuff picked me up a bit.

In September, Mom took me back to see Dr. Buccha at Harvey's Lake Veterinary Hospital, where he and Mom discussed my condition. Dr. Buccha said my kidney numbers had only improved slightly, showing that I did indeed have kidney disease. This was a great disappointment to Mom and me, but we had to accept the fact that I needed to remain on the fluids.

Mom was particularly concerned about the effect all my medications were having on my kidneys. I needed these medications to breathe, but they were not what a cat with failing kidneys should be taking. Dr. Buccha told Mom an inhaler might be better for me. It could stop an asthma attack in its tracks. He had a small mask just my size, which could be used with an inhaler. Dr. Buccha said whenever I started to have a problem, Mom should shake the inhaler, put it in the mask piece, and put the mask over my face. Then, while holding it firmly in place, she had to pump the inhaler twice and count to ten before removing it.

My first experiences with this were really awful. When Mom put the mask over my face, I thought I wasn't going to be able to breathe at all, and I struggled to take it off. However, Mom kept insisting that I try it and rubbed my diaphragm to help me relax. After several times, I realized that by using the mask, the asthma attack would stop, and I would be able to breathe again. So, in time, I learned to accept it.

In mid-September, Mom took us cats back to New Jersey for a few days, but this trip was very confusing for me. Instead of staying at our old apartment, we stayed in the house next door. It was the house with the garden where I used to wander when Mom took me out for air. Our neighbor, Aurora, lived upstairs and she let us stay in her apartment downstairs. The apartment also had a garden in the back.

When we were visiting, Mom took me out to the back garden several times a day so I could wander. Inside the apartment, however, it was so dusty and dirty (partly from the construction next door) that it set my asthma off. Soon, I was coughing and wheezing worse than ever. I wondered why we couldn't just go back up to our old apartment. Mom set a fan in the window to blow fresh air in, and this helped a little.

Perhaps my mom didn't know just how sad and confused I felt at this time. Most of my days there were spent curled up on a pillow, trying to sleep away my sorrow. When at last we returned to White Haven, I was glad.

The last few months had indeed taken their toll on me. In May, I weighed 9.4 pounds, which was the most I had ever weighed in my life. By mid-September, however, when we stopped at the Animal Clinic of Jersey City on our way home, I weighed in at 7.4 pounds. That was a huge loss, perhaps partly due to my kidney disease.

Shortly after this, Mom bought me some special kidney diet biscuits (we always called out dry food "biscuits"), and I loved them. Someone also suggested baby food for me. Since I needed a low protein diet, Mom began buying some baby food chicken dinners and mixing in the pureed chicken and vegetables. I acquired a real taste for those meals. They were so much easier to eat than canned cat food. Later, we had to stop using some of these foods as Mom learned they had onion powder in them, and onion powder is something cats should not have. We also learned that baby food does not have all the nutrients a cat needs.

As the leaves began to fall in White Haven, our house was filled with boxes and other things from New Jersey. It was not the pretty or peaceful place it had been. Instead, it was a crowded maze I had to wander through to find the bathroom and bedroom.

Then, at the end of October, Mom said, "Winter is coming. We're going back to Tennessee."

❧

Once again, the car was packed, and we cats were put in our cages. This time, I hissed at Mom. I had had enough of all this traveling and I really didn't feel like getting in that car in my cage under all the junk she piled in with us.

To make me happier and more secure, Mom put my cage in the middle of the back seat where the ride would be a little less bumpy. From this spot, I could easily see Mom, and she could see me. Once we were out on the road with the fresh air and sunshine, I began to feel somewhat better. Most of the time, though, I slept. I was much more tired these days than I had been in the past.

The new complication of our travel was that I had to be sure to get my fluids every day. I also needed to have them at a time when I could be near my toilet box because shortly after receiving them, I would have to (excuse me) pee a lot. So, Mom began to give me my fluids at night, and just to make sure I had enough fluids in the day, she would spoon-feed me water.

On this journey, we traveled directly south from Pennsylvania into Maryland, West Virginia, Virginia, and then Tennessee. Time on the road seemed to fly quickly, but I would like to recount one story along the way.

When we first got into Tennessee, Mom saw a Knights Inn, and since we had stayed at the Knights Inn in Murfreesboro, she stopped there. The only room available was upstairs. Mom was too tired to drive anymore, so she took it and carted us and all our stuff up the stairs. Of course, when they asked at the desk if she had any pets, she told them "no."

The next morning, when Mom went in to pay the bill, the woman who ran the motel said, "And you have a ket."

"No," Mom told her, "I don't have a cat."

"Yes," the woman said, "You have a leetle, white ket with da gray. My husband see it sitting in da window."

So, what could Mom say? She paid the additional ten dollars, thankful they didn't know about the rest of us. But, for the remainder of our trip, Mom kept telling Pennsy, "You cost me ten dollars today! Stay out of the window!" We were low on money, and those ten dollars meant a lot.

We arrived in Murfreesboro that evening, and I was relieved to see we were staying in the same house we had stayed the previous year. Not feeling so well, it made things a lot easier to be on familiar ground.

⟡

Mom and I were hopeful that I might feel better here, and not have the terrible lung irritation I'd had during the past year in Pennsylvania. October was still warm in Tennessee, so even though most of the windows in the house didn't open, Mom fixed a fan just inside the front screen door, and in the evenings, we had fresh air blowing throughout the house. She also fixed a box in front of the door, where we cats could take turns sitting and looking out.

I felt good to start, but a few weeks later, the weather turned cold, and we had to keep the door closed. I had already felt some irritation in the air, but now I began to feel terribly ill. The strange thing was I had never had any problems in this house before. This time, however, there was definitely something in the air. My throat felt scratchy and so did my chest. A few days later, I began to have heaving attacks. My sides would go in and out, as I opened my mouth, gasping for air, but I could not seem to catch my breath. As I attempted to breathe, there was also a terrible noise coming from my throat.

Seeing me like this, Mom was horrified. She said I sounded like I had the croup. The worst thing was that we had very little money, even for food. I did go once to the South Church Street Animal Hospital, where the very nice vet gave me some antibiotics and nose drops, but this barely seemed to help me.

In the following weeks, Mom got a job, but like most jobs in Murfreesboro, it didn't pay the kind of money we needed to cover our bills. During the next month, one of the church kitchens donated a good supply of food to Mom, and our dear friend, Curry, lent us money. This helped us to survive. Still, our visits to the vet had to be few and far between.

The most important thing was to make sure I had my fluids and my medications. Mom ordered my fluids through the mail, and begged the vet to give me my pills without the usual cost of an office visit. Finally, she found that Murfreesboro Animal Clinic would fill my prescriptions, after I had one visit. Still, I know she cut back on her meals to make sure there was money for my pills. "It's okay," she told me, "I needed to lose weight anyway!"

During that winter, there were so many late nights when I was down on the floor, bent over, trying to catch my breath. This time around, the pills and the inhaler helped only so much. Besides, I was only supposed to use the inhaler once a day, or twice at most, and with the condition of my kidneys, Mom was afraid of over-medicating me. The doctors all said I should use my pills very "sparingly."

From November to March, there were only two things—aside from leaving the house—that really helped stop my attacks. One was when Mom put me on her shoulder like a baby, bouncing me up and down a bit, and patting my back. This helped to stop the convulsing of my lungs.

The other thing Mom did was make a big pot of hot water (sometimes she'd put Vicks on my nose, which I hated!) and put me under a towel while she held my head above the pot and steamed me. I really didn't like this, but at a certain point my condition was so bad I didn't have a choice. She also rubbed my tummy during this treatment to try to relax my diaphragm and ease my breathing. For a while, I got these treatments first thing in the morning, and then once or twice at night. They really helped to soothe my lungs.

All that winter, Mom was constantly giving me all kinds of vitamins, teas, and herbal medicines. I had peppermint tea with honey, mullein tea, golden seal tea, herbal allergy drops, and many other things. Mom was always reading up on something new, like rosemary tea, which was supposed to sooth my "membranes," whatever that meant! I took everything she gave me, although some of it, like Quercetin, made me gag. Once in a while, I'd get so mad that I'd take my paw with a claw out and push her hand away. Believe me, when I had had enough, I knew what to do. She was trying to help me, but sometimes it just got to be too much. I think she knew that because then she would say, "Okay, Sabrina, I'm just going to let you be. Feel better, baby."

My mom did so many good things for me. She cooked chicken and veg-etables, and whipped the whole thing up in the blender, so I could eat it easily. Then, she would comb me and give me Shiatsu. And every night, she slept with her hand right next to me, so she could feel if I was okay. She woke up several times a night to check on me, and if I showed the slightest discomfort, she got up and tried to help me.

Mom also kept the vaporizer going for me, and this seemed to help as well. One time, she tried to tack a sheet up to the wall, to make a little tent over my portion of the bed, with vaporizer under it. I really liked being under that tent; somehow the air felt better. But then, the sheet got all wet and the wall did too; so, Mom had to take it down.

By now, we had figured out that the air in the room was toxic, but we didn't know why. Mom was always cleaning, so, there wouldn't be any dust. The real clue about the air was that whenever I got under a sheet or blanket, I could breathe much better. Once I discovered this, I stated going under the blankets on my own. Mom often came home to find either my face, or my entire body under the covers. Then, whenever I went to sleep, Mom started covering me up with a baby blanket I'd had since kittenhood so my breathing wouldn't be irritated by whatever was in the room.

Eventually, Mom thought she understood why I had gotten so ill. It seems while we were away, some people had stayed in the house and brought their dogs with them. When they left, the house was so full of fleas Mom's friends, Aleesha and Joel, had to bomb the place twice to get rid of them. Following that, they shampooed the carpets twice, but Mom was certain that, in my delicate condition, I was being affected by the remnants of this poison.

Now, Mom took me out of the house whenever she could. In fact, I went out riding nearly every day. Our trips were usually short, but one day, when Mom was especially concerned about me, she took me to work for half a day. This was a little too long for me. When Mom finally showed up after four hours, I let her know that she had made me really anxious!

Every Sunday, I went to church. When the weather was warmer, I had to stay in my cage so the windows could be put down part way. However,

With Pennsy's help, Theo and I made peace

if the weather was cool enough, the windows would only be cracked, and I was allowed to get out of my cage and roam around the car, or sleep in the sun on Mom's seat. After church, I'd climb back in my cage, and we'd go home.

I got so used to going out with Mom that riding in the car became one of my great pleasures. I used to purr when Mom took me out, and I always knew when we were nearing home. I liked the independence of getting in and out of my cage on my own, as well as jumping out of the car, and walking up to the porch, nibbling grass along the way. There was a kind of respect and trust between my Mom and me, and that made me feel good.

In Murfreesboro, my favorite time of day was when Mom came home for lunch, which she did nearly every day. On nice days, she'd take me out on the front porch, and the two of us would sit there in the sun, enjoying the day. Even on most winter days in Tennessee, you can still sit outside in the mid-day sun and feel good.

Somehow we braved through the winter. During this time, Theo and Pennsy were pretty good to me. Sometimes, when I really didn't feel well,

Pennsy would come and sleep next to me, trying to make me feel better. I always liked him, and I appreciated his desire to comfort me. Once in while, Mom still catches me smiling at him.

🐱

By March, Mom had saved a little money, and she made an appointment to get my blood tested at one of the local vets we had seen in the past. When you have a kidney condition, you are supposed to take a blood test now and then, just to watch your levels and make sure you are getting enough fluids.

So, Mom and I went into the office, and after the vet had taken my blood and examined me she said, "Well, her blood volume has gone down a little. You know with kidney patients when the blood goes down, the marrow can't produce red blood cells. They get tired and short of breath. She's on her way there. She's okay now, but by May you should start thinking about putting her down. She's been a good kitty and you don't want her to suffer."

Mom didn't say much after that. She put me in the cage, paid the bill, and took me out to the car. By now, I was feeling a little better than I had in previous months. I couldn't believe what I had just heard. It went through me like a knife. In two months, Mom was supposed to take me to die? What was my Mom thinking? She hadn't said anything; she hadn't even looked at me.

Mom put my cage in the center of the back seat and strapped it in. When, she got in her seat up front, she turned to look at me, and our eyes met. I was feeling so distressed at that moment, that I didn't know what to think. Mom had done so many things the vets told her. Would she do this too? I guess all my thoughts were there in my eyes. Without words, I was asking her: "You would do this to me? You would kill me?" I felt terrified and utterly betrayed.

Mom took one look at me and said, "Oh, Sabrina, I would never do that to you. Honey, don't worry. Don't pay any attention to that vet. You never have to come back here again."

Well, that was good to hear, but I so shaken by the vet's words, I couldn't get over them. People don't realize that animals understand what is said. It was bad enough that I had not been feeling too well, but I didn't think it was any reason to kill me! In the past, the vets had always said good things about me—how beautiful I was, how strong, how amazing. This one just said I shouldn't suffer; I should die.

That night, when Mom and I were sitting on the bed with the heater going, I approached her again, looking up into her face. I wanted to be certain of how she really felt. I had simply never heard anything like what that vet said. Each time I looked at my mom, she rubbed my head and kissed me, saying, "Oh, Sabrina! Mommy loves you. Don't worry, honey. We are never going back to that vet again. Mom will never do that. I promise. I will always be with you no matter what happens."

Finally, after many reassurances from my mom, we snuggled together. Mom slept with her face up against me while I purred happily.

"You're my girl, Sabrina," Mom told me. And then, we played the tail-tap game. One-two-three taps by Mom, and one-two-three taps of the tail by me.

$$\mathfrak{z}$$

A week or so later, a miracle occurred. Mom received a check from her friend, Barbara, for my care. Barbara wrote me a beautiful note, telling me she wanted me to have this money in memory of her own beloved dog, Fuzzy.

Shortly before this, Mom had heard about a very good holistic vet up in Brentwood, Tennessee. So now, only weeks after being told I should die, and one month before my 19th birthday, Mom and I headed up to Brentwood for a visit with Dr. Mark Ingram at the Franklin Road Animal Hospital.

Dr. Ingram examined me and then asked if he could do a test on me using "kinesiology." This test involved someone putting one hand on me, while they held various remedies for illnesses with the other hand. The doctor then tried to push the hand of the person holding the remedy down in order to see how strong the reaction was. I was told to relax, so I just sat there quietly through half an hour of testing.

In the end, the doctor prescribed something to perk up my system, and some remedies for allergies. Dr. Ingram also told Mom that I seemed to want a remedy for my heart. No doctor had ever told Mom I needed something for my heart, so at first she hesitated. We only had limited money to spend, and this was a consideration. Then, just before we left, Mom decided she would buy the heart supplement as well.

Dr. Ingram told Mom I was very fragile and should not have any more immunizations. He also said I should live a very quiet life. He thought that with care, I could get stronger, but said my condition was very guarded.

While we were at the Franklin Road Animal Hospital, Mom learned about Dr. Ingram's suggested diet for healthy pets. As a holistic vet, he believed animal diets should be as close to what we would eat in the wild as possible. The prescribed diet was one meal of raw organic meat and one meal of raw vegetables. No grains. Dr. Ingram told Mom the best thing for my allergies would be lots of raw, organic chicken.

Mom said she felt some uncertainty about this because she had always heard that kidney patients are supposed to have low-protein diets. Dr. Ingram said I was so thin now (I was down to 7.0 pounds), that it was more important for me to get good nutrition. On the way home, Mom stopped at Fresh Farms in Franklin and bought me some raw organic chicken parts. I can tell you, as bad as my illness had been, and as small as my appetite was, when I got home, boy, did I enjoy that raw chicken. I not only ate what Mom gave me, I wanted more!

In the coming months, Mom also bought me some little pieces of raw organic steak. She would singe them slightly on each side to kill any organisms, and then, slice them into very tiny pieces. Sometimes, she even put the steak into the blender and ground it up. After my first meal of this raw steak, it became my new passion! Organic chicken and steak (chicken especially) are nothing like the regular chicken and beef you buy at the store. They are really great! Still, Mom wanted to be cautious with this diet, so I didn't get it all the time.

Along with this new diet, there was a lot of medication for me to take. Most important of all was something called "Body Balance." I had to take two full droppers of this, twice a day. This was to add nutrients to my body. Body Balance is something people can take too.

Over the last months, my illnesses and pill taking had really depleted me. Not only was I thin and scrawny, but my coat had become dull and rough. I was losing the fur on my ears and even my head. Along with this, of course, I had become extremely exhausted. I could barely stay awake at all, and fell into deep sleeps most of the time. I had never been in such terrible condition. I was like an old woman waiting to die.

In the two weeks following my visit with Dr. Ingram, faithfully taking his advice and remedies, my coat became shiny and beautiful again. I also began to gain weight. I was staying awake and much more aware of my surroundings. I even began cleaning myself again. It felt like a miracle.

It seemed as if life could have gone on as it was, indefinitely, right there in Tennessee. It was perfect, but we all knew one day we would have to go back to Pennsylvania. Mom was in serious financial trouble. We had a house full of belongings in White Haven, while the nearly empty house in Tennessee could be rented easily. So a month after my first visit with Dr. Ingram, and with our few possessions sold, Mom rented the house, packed the car, and off we went to Pennsylvania.

This time, the trip home was without detour. Mom had no money, and she knew, despite the fact that I was feeling better, I had little strength to waste.

Chapter 25
Peaceful Days

When we arrived in Pennsylvania, it was spring. The trees had just turned pale green, the wild flowers were blooming, and all was fresh and clean.

At the entrance to our community, Mom opened the door to my cage, and I climbed up front with her, seating myself on her lap. As we rode slowly down the private lanes toward our house, I was so excited looking out the window at all the dear, familiar woods. Then, as we came up the hill and turned into our driveway, I began to purr madly.

How happy I was when the car stopped, and Mom let me down outside. I walked up the hill to our house, munching grass along the way. For me, the last months had been a long, hard journey, but now I was home!

At home in White Haven, I can relax. My travels are over, and I know I want to spend my final days in this place—my beloved home. To me, it is the most beautiful place in the world.

Since we returned to White Haven, Mom has kept the air filter going most of the time, along with the vaporizer and the fan. We have found that the fan helps my breathing problems a lot. Keeping the air circulating prevents those terrible asthma attacks that take all my strength.

My first year in White Haven, I ran and leapt in the air with joy. My second year, I walked and ran around the house. Now, each morning when Mom puts me out on the porch to get fresh air, I simply sit by the door and look out at the land beyond. My eyes are not good and my steps are not too steady, so I don't like to wander far. Sometimes, I walk around the deck, and look at the distant lands. Then, I wait at the door for Mom to let me in.

On occasion, if Mom is outside, I am bold enough to walk all the way around the house. This includes walking down a little hill, around the garage wall, and back up the hill to the steps and the front door. It is an interesting trip. I look for all the familiar spots—the ferns, the grass and the flowers.

I still remember the day I met a deer. I stood stock still looking at her, and she stood stock still looking at me. That was when my mother saw us about ten feet apart. She didn't know what was going to happen, and with a little fear in her voice, she called, "Sabrina!" Then the deer ran off, and I returned to Mom. That was one of the most exciting moments in my life because I knew I was in the presence of true wildlife!

Sometimes, when Mom is not working, she and I will ride down to the lake. We'll lie there together on a bench in the sun—just she and I. It is beautiful and peaceful there with all the green grass and the smooth lake reflecting the sky. After we lie there for a while, it's my instinct to get down and wander across the big lawn. Mom keeps me on the bench though. She thinks it's good for my lungs to get fresh air and sunshine.

I still get baths now and then. Mom thinks they are good for me too. Having kidney disease, my fur can get very oily, and I don't always have the strength to wash myself very well. Mom says the bath hydrates me. However, now when I take a bath, it's in the kitchen sink, not the tub. Mom washes me very quickly with a little water and liquid Castile soap. Then, she pours a few cups of water over my back, so as not to stress me, and wraps me in a special towel that is made to absorb water.

Last summer, Mom sent me outside after a bath, and I wandered down the driveway to a sunny spot where I licked myself dry. My fur was awfully soft and clean after that bath. The bath did help.

It is not easy to grow old, but I try to enjoy each day as it comes. I am grateful for the beauty that surrounds me, and even for the companionship of my old enemy, Theo, and the young Pennsy. And I am grateful for the love and companionship of my mother. I know I can trust her to give me the best of care. "Sabrina stuck by me, through all the difficult times," she says. "Now I will stick by her."

In recent months, my back legs have gotten weak, but I can still hop up the steps to the front door. Even more so, to my own pride, I can still jump up to my seat on the sofa.

After nineteen years together, I no longer sleep in the bedroom with Mom. She says that's okay because the air isn't as good in the bedroom. These days, I prefer the wide-open space of the living room where I can vary my resting places between the chair with the red and black plaid wool blanket and the sofa with the pillow for my head. I like to change my locations now and then.

In the living room, there is nice bowl of water on the table next to my chair. Mom put it up on a plastic cookie container, just as she did for my food. That way I don't have to bend over. In the daytime, I can eat and drink from the stand, while I look out the window at the land, the trees, the deer and the squirrels. I love my view!

There's more water down where Pennsy and Theo eat, and a toilet box near by. I can also sit on the platform by the big glass door. That's where the scratching post is. Sometimes, I nap there in the sun.

All this is my home, and I'm comfortable here to do what I want and enjoy myself. I am the queen of my home. There is no doubt about that in anyone's mind. Mom defers to me, and usually the boys do too. Above all, I know I am loved, and I know that I love. God has blessed me with a long and interesting life, and a mother who always has and always will love me.

Chapter 26
A Little More Time . . .

Mom broke her elbow last August; so, except for one day in the hospital, she has been home with us for the last three months. It has been an odd sort of time. She has been there for us, but barely able to take care of herself. We all stay together in the living room. Mom sleeps on the couch, while I sleep on my chair, just across from her. Sometimes, I even sleep on the foot of the couch with her. She keeps either the fan or the air filter running all the time, and that helps my breathing.

In November, for Thanksgiving, we all traveled upstate New York to visit Mom's friends, Tom and Marie Hegeman. We had a room all to ourselves on the second floor of the Hegeman home. One day during our visit, I was actually able to go outside in the sun and wander about.

Last week, which was the beginning of December, we took one more trip down to New Jersey. Since we couldn't stay with our old neighbor, Aurora, we spent one night in a motel and two nights in the extra room of Mom's friend, Werner. That trip was very difficult for me. I was so tired and miserable, I could barely move, but I made it though. I was grateful when we got home again. There is nothing like being home when you don't feel well.

Once again, I have grown thin and weak. I know Mom has tried to research the help I need, but no one really seems to know. I take my medicines and my vitamins—so many of them—every day. I always try to do what Mom asks. I hope, as much as she does, that these things will make me feel better. In the past, everything she did for me helped. But now I know that, sadly, I am failing. My spirit wishes to live, but my body cannot keep up. So, I spend most of my time sleeping.

When she can, Mom still takes me in the car with her. I have gone to Mountain Top with her several times, where she gets her physical therapy. I also go to the store when she goes shopping. Our rides are over peaceful hills and valleys. I guess Mom thinks it will perk me up to go out in the car, but I tire so very quickly these days. While Mom is inside doing her therapy or shopping, I get into her seat and sleep in the sun. My favorite part of going out is when we come home again. At the entrance of our little community, I get to come out of my cage and ride on her lap. Even when I'm so very tired, and Mom has to support me with one hand, I hang on to the top of the door and look at everything I can. I just love it. Then, when we turn up the hill, that is most exciting of all, for I know when we get to the top, we will see my house. Despite all of my illnesses, it is still really my favorite thing to do.

⁊

Last week, I was struck by sudden weakness. It is difficult for me to walk now, but my mother is patient with me, and Pennsy and Theo do not bother me. I like to sit in my chair by the window. From there, I can easily see both the living room and the outdoors. In two steps, I can be up on the stand where my water sits. Mom even made a toilet box for me with one side down so I don't have to lift my legs to get into it. At least, I can still have my dignity.

It is not easy being old, but the beauty of the country and the love of my family surround me. At times, my mother takes me outdoors, putting my new, little, blue coat and my red boots on because, she says, I need to keep warm. Once in a while, even with my weak legs, I take my old walk around the house, just to see what's what, and to search for grass, and remember where I once saw the deer, and she saw me.

Now that I am too tired to eat sometimes, my mother puts a bib on me and feeds me. I know she is trying hard, and I am trying hard too, but my body is just not up to doing all the things I would like it to do. It makes me sad, but I look in Mom's eyes and try to find hope. I know she loves me, and I want to get well for her.

When my mother is most worried about me, she talks to me about heaven. There, she says, I will meet my long lost daughter, Elizabeth, my granddaughter, Blossom, and her mother, Marian. She says that God has made a place for us cats. I am not quite ready to go yet, but I know the day is coming. Then, when I am so very weary and weak, and feel so alone, my mother holds me on her chest, and we sleep together, heart to heart.

Epilogue

My dear little girl, Sabrina, hung on for a long time, but in December, she had some kind of collapse, and her back legs became weak. I wish I had known more clearly long before this that her heart needed attention. However, many of the vets we saw wrote her off because of her age and kidney disease. Other than our holistic vet, no one ever suggested checking her heart, or giving her treatment for it.

With the help of her steroid pills, Sabrina had enough strength to get up, use her toilet box, and go to her food. Toward the end of the year, she seemed to rally a bit. I followed her desires in allowing her to stay home and be cared for by us.

Just after New Year's Day, on January 2nd, 2007 at 5 AM, Sabrina left us. She was listening to her dear Nancy LaMott sing, surrounded by her cat family, and the prayers and love of her mother. We pray that she has gone to the beautiful garden God has prepared for all good animals, where there is no more illness or pain. Sabrina Russell lived a brave life and, with her wonderful personality, taught us many lessons. She earned her reward, and we thank the Lord for the blessing of her presence in our lives these nearly twenty years.

I think of Sabrina every day, and I know when I reach heaven, I will see her waiting there among God's angels.

> *"And God will wipe away every tear from their eyes;*
> *there shall be no more death, nor sorrow . . ."*
> Revelations 21:4

Sabrina's Jewish Chicken Soup

1 whole chicken
3 carrots, sliced
1 stalk of celery, sliced finely
¼ teaspoon rosemary
a pinch of thyme
finely chopped parsley (optional)
1 zucchini with thick slices (if you like)

Clean the chicken (wash inside & out with salt, then rinse). Cut out all fat & scrape the skin to take off any excess fat. Put chicken in pot with enough water to almost cover it and turn to medium heat. Once bubbling, skim off excess fat or residue, then lower heat.

When chicken is partially cooked, or after approximately ½ hour, add celery and carrots. (Make sure to break or slice celery stalk and pull strings off.) Once boiling, reduce heat to low. Add rosemary and thyme. Cover pot and let simmer for 1 hour or more until meat is coming off bones. After about 1 hour, add parsley. Cook 15 minutes more, until done.

Cut enough chicken for one small cat meal, mash carrots and add soup into saucer (flat dish makes it easer to cool, but you need a lip so the liquid doesn't spill). Let cool to just warm before serving. You may also add water to cool.

NOTE: Refrigerate chicken & soup whole. A layer of yellow fat will form. Remove it from portion you reheat. We have found that organic chicken has very little fat.

You may choose to cook chicken with only carrots, which we often do, or some other vegetables edible for cats. You may also use chicken parts such as thighs (dark meat is best), however a whole chicken provides the greatest nutrition.

DISCLAIMER: It has been found that onions and garlic may cause serious health problems in cats—including leukemia and blood clots, so this recipe has been revised from Sabrina's original. Anitra Frazier, originally a proponent of garlic for cats, has recently changed the information in her *The New Natural Cat* book.

Bibliography

The New Natural Cat: A Complete Guide for Finicky Owners, by Anitra Frazier with Norma Eckroate, A Dutton Book, 1990

Appendix

The following recordings were listened to by Sabrina, and referred to in this book:

Doris Day, Golden Girl, Sony Entertainment, Inc., 1999

Nancy LaMott recordings:

Beautiful Baby, Midder Music, 1991

Come Rain or Come Shine, Songs of Johnny Mercer, 1992

My Foolish Heart, Midder Music, 1993

Listen To My Heart, Midder Music Records, 1995

What's Good About Goodbye, Midder Music Records, Inc.

Michelle Russell & The Moonlight Band, 2001

Barbra Streisand, Higher Ground, Sony Music, Entertainment, Inc., 1997 (contains the song "On Holy Ground")

Un-Reconstructed, 2003

Home Sweet Home, Cumberland Records.

Index

Catsong Publishing
Order Form

To order online with a credit card, please go to http://www.catsongpublishing.com

Quantity   Books

_____   **Sabrina—The Autobiography of a Cat** $12.95

_____   **Sabrina** *original edition* $7.95

_____   **A Cat Named Toto** (children's book) $7.95

_____   **Meet Lily—A Very Little Girl** (children's book) $10.95

_____   **From Tennessee to Oz, Part 1** (1793–1870) $19.95
           The Amazing Saga of Judy Garland's Family History

_____   **From Tennessee to Oz, Part 2** (1870–1943) $24.95
           The Amazing Saga of Judy Garland's Family History

Quantity   Music Recording

_____   **Made in America—22 Vaudeville Songs CD** $12.95
           Songs Judy Garland's family sang when she was a child, performed by a cast of five

Prices include postage. *Discount of $3.50 for 3 or more items. Discount not available for original* Sabrina *edition and/or children's books exclusively.*

Discount   _____

MN residents please add sales tax   _____

Total   _____

Mail order form (or photocopy) and payment to:

Catsong Publishing
33034 Crystal Springs Road
Grand Rapids, MN 55744

www.ingramcontent.com/pod-product-compliance
Lightning Source LLC
LaVergne TN
LVHW011156080426
835508LV00007B/438